FORGET CARTER

THE FILMS AND TELEVISION OF NEWCASTLE

CHRIS PHIPPS

Tyne
Bridge
Publishing

Published by:
City of Newcastle Upon Tyne
Newcastle Libraries
Tyne Bridge Publishing, 2016
www.tynebridgepublishing.co.uk

Design: David Hepworth

Front cover: *Images from the Newcastle collection.*
Title page: *The Odeon Cinema, Pilgrim Street.*

In memory of Peggy Phipps, Winston Phipps and Gary Holton

This book is dedicated to Diane And Miriam

CINEMA IS PISH POSH FOR PEOPLE WITH
PROLETARIAN MINDS.

Newcastle Cinema Owner

THE CINEMA HAS BECOME TO US WHAT THE
AEROPAGUS WAS TO ATHENS OR THE FORUM TO
ROME.

Frank Evans [aka Ernest Dyer]
Film Critic Evening Chronicle, 1936

Opening Credits

A city can embody social history, struggle, architectural ambition, power and corruption.

Cities have dominated my life - a bombed out Birmingham in the 50s, a Bournville workers' estate in the 60s and, as a young BBC reporter, the 'smouldering carpet' that was the Black Country.

I came to Newcastle to work in television over three decades ago. As I stepped off the train in Central Station I couldn't avoid feeling like Jack Carter, a tribute perhaps to the power of Mike Hodges' 1971 imagery. I would walk along a deserted and derelict Quayside every morning to Tyne Tees Television on City Road. From the canteen, in hectic moments you could stare at the ventilators revolving on the roof of the Baltic Flour Mill, like giant birds or reptiles.

This book explores how Newcastle upon Tyne and the region it embodies has been a leading player on the big and small screens of our lives. The city has always been there, a concrete backdrop to Jack Carter's revenge, new build estates for the Likely Lads' social mobility musings, a bridge to frame Tosker's ambitions in *Our Friends in the North*, Oz's hopes in *Auf Wiedersehen Pet*, the Reality TV gang of *Geordie Shore* - and to greet *Vera* as she contemplates her next case.

In the controversial words of J.B. Priestley, 'Newcastle - a place of sombre dignity?'

Long Stairs, 1962.

Foreword

A key creation of the New Labour government was the UK Film Council, charged with building a world-class UK film industry. As part of this initiative UKFC set up a nine-strong network of Screen Agencies to serve the regions of England with Northern Film & Media (NFM) created to cover the North East.

With a funding allocation from UKFC, the Regional Development Agency network and in some cases EU funds, the Screen Agencies could set about developing the media industry in the regions with unprecedented levels of funding.

Amongst a variety of functions including audience development, exhibition, media literacy and training, NFM was also responsible for providing direct investment in the development of the region's practitioners and their projects and productions. NFM also carried on the successful work of the Northern Screen Commission in attracting filming to the region and promoting local crew and facilities.

Investment in individual feature films was never on the scale of the UKFC nationally, but we always strived to make sure that NFM's contribution made a difference, moved a project forward or formed a crucial building block in the precarious business of financing a film.

One such investment was Stone City Films' Bryn Higgins-directed feature *Unconditional* shot entirely in the North East with Newcastle figuring prominently. This thought-provoking drama exploring the relationship between a loan shark and a customer's teenage twin children might never have been financed without the high-risk money provided by NFM. A hit at the 2012 Edinburgh International, it would certainly never have been filmed in the North East without it.

Two personal favourites are football feature film, 2005's *Goal!* and shoot-'em-up action thriller *The Tournament* released in 2009 - every seven years a competition to find the world's top hitman or woman is held – who knew? – and this time it's in Middlesbrough, the town with the greatest concentration of CCTV in the UK. A couple of techies tap into these cameras to allow a group of billionaire gamblers to bet on the contest whilst watching the unfolding action live on the big screen in a secret Middlesbrough location. With a reported $8m budget it's got the lot, killings, explosions, car chases, and a nine-strong hitman shoot out in a local strip club. Written by Jonathan Frank, Gary Young (*Harry Brown*) and Nick Rowntree, who each make excellent cameo appearances, with Young particularly hilarious as the headphone-wearing garage attendant unaware of the mayhem going on behind him while he microwaves his supper. Directed by Scott Mann who went on to direct Robert De Niro in 2015's *Heist*, who could resist Ving Rhames killing a rival competitor in the iconic *Get Carter* car park or Robert Carlyle, an alcoholic failed priest, getting thrown out of the William IV pub on Gateshead High Street?

Goal! was a different kettle of fish, a genuine studio project, it didn't need our money, but we did lend office space and a lot of production support. Telling the story of Santiago, a talented LA based illegal immigrant Mexican footballer who miraculously finds himself on a month's trial at Newcastle United's rain-soaked training ground, the film plots the ups and downs of his time on Tyneside. A genuine feel-good film, Newcastle United, including bit-part player Alan Shearer, must win the final three games of the season to qualify for the Champions League (not as preposterous in 2005 as it sounds now). I won't spoil the film by telling you the rest, as if you couldn't guess, but I would urge you to beg steal or hire a copy of this little gem, and the rest of the films featured in Chris's book.

More recently Ken Loach shot his 2016 Cannes Palme D'Or winner *I, Daniel Blake* in Newcastle, proof of the city's, and indeed the North East's, enduring appeal as a location for filming. And I haven't even mentioned numerous appearances as a backdrop to forty years' worth of popular TV drama.

Following the 2010 coalition government's decision to abolish the Film Council the network of Regional Screen Agencies is no more, but Northern Film & Media remains, for now at least, to support the region's filmmakers, just without the grant funding. We still promote the region for filmmaking, (*Transformers* coming soon!) and develop talent and advocate for film and TV businesses who wish to remain in this fantastic, if under-served far-flung corner of the UK film industry.

John Tulip
Managing Director
Northern Film & Media Limited

Diana Wynyard and Ralph Richarson - pipe and accordion.

On the Night of the Fire (1940)

Produced 1939, released 1940
USA Title: *The Fugitive*
Ralph Richardson as Will Kobling
Diana Wynyard as Mrs Kobling
Glynys Johns as a maid
Irene Handl as a local gossip
Henry Oscar as Pillager
Directed by Brian Desmond Hurst
From the book by F. C. Green

On the Night of the Fire, is a 1939 film that has perhaps gone under the radar, to use a well-worn expression - yet it is perhaps the film equivalent of an iceberg in its position and influence on British Cinema. Dominating this dark drama is Newcastle upon Tyne. There, in the opening shot is the Tyne Bridge, filmed from Northumberland County Hall, which today is the Vermont Hotel. Ralph Richardson, as the socially dissatisfied barber Will Kobling, watches the steamer *Scandinavia* head for Dunston from his position on the Swing Bridge. This leads to establishing shots of his wife, baby and maid in their humble surroundings.

En route home, possibly on a street near Dog Leap Stairs, Will looks through an open office window and spies a pile of money left unguarded. Unable to resist temptation, he climbs through the window to steal the cash, before returning home. This small act of theft unleashes a tragic trail of events for Will and his family.

Next, we glimpse Will and his wife enjoying a saunter through the Quayside Sunday market, complacent with his clandestine riches. This picturesque and comfortable atmosphere will mutate as the plot unravels into something dark and fatal for those involved.

The stolen money is used by Kobling to pay off his wife's secret debts to a conniving draper named Pillager. Pillager then attempts to blackmail Kobling over the real source of the stolen money. When a huge fire breaks out in the dockside street, the local community is evacuated, which enables Kobling to confront the draper before he has the chance to leave the shop. During this altercation, Kobling murders Pillager and the runes are cast – 'on the night of the fire'.

Kobling's fate is sealed and his life, and that of his family, spirals into tragedy as the police pursue him around Newcastle before the final showdown.

Curiously, Newcastle is never actually named in the film, though there is a glimpse of a newspaper called the *Northern Chronicle*. The colourful, sharp-featured supporting cast of characters are not caricatures as was usual at this time in British films, when the working class was normally portrayed as music hall parodies. Not so in this movie, there is an attempt at realism amongst a tightly-knit and watchful community, united by the fire and the subsequent murder amongst them.

There are few Geordie accents. Richardson and Wynyard have lower middle class 'cut-glass' accents, the barber's boy is straight out of the Oliver Twist 'guvnor' school of acting. Accents range from Cockney to Yorkshire and only the leader of the local vigilantes attempts a Geordie accent.

In some ways Ralph Richardson is playing a working class 'everyman' living in a fictionalised setting of 'everycity' - and he plays it well.

Much of the film has a theatrical, claustrophobic atmosphere. The studio sets are very effective. Kobling's barber shop and the dingy drapers are in a huge studio set clearly based upon the bottom of Dean Street and Akenside. The location exteriors include Wallsend, Byker, the Tyne Bridge, the Swing Bridge, Dog Leap Stairs and the Quayside Sunday market.

When Kobling is being shadowed by detectives, there is a stunning sequence by Ouseburn Viaduct as Kobling visits a small shop to seek a cleaner. The shop was listed as No. 2, Ouseburn Road owned by Mary Anne Hastings. It was reported locally that local boy, Bob Phillips, was paid threepence to run across Crawford's Bridge for the film. There are also shots of the old Paint Works - now Byker Farm. Critics have said locations in Lambeth and Southwark were also used. A key question about *On the Night of the Fire* is why, in those pre-war days where film studios would seek low production costs, did the production crew choose to travel to Newcastle? The answer may lie with Brian Desmond Hurst, a maverick director who had made the first sound film in Northern Ireland and trained under John Ford in California. As a boy Hurst had lived in poverty in Ireland, where his itinerant shipyard father had travelled to Belfast, Scotland and possibly Newcastle in search of ship labour. This experience may have influenced Hurst's choice of location in 1939. His comments to the local press during filming in 1939 were flattering – '*THE most filmic city I have been in - all those bridges - why hasn't it been used before?*'

It is interesting to note that Hurst was involved in the John Ford epic *The Informer* which has a similar theme to *On the Night of the Fire* - a man suspected by his own community of an act of betrayal. After this film, Hurst would go on to direct classics like *Dangerous Moonlight* and *A Christmas Carol*.

Another answer to the mysterious choice of location may lie with the author of the original book, F. C. Green. Green was also the author of the classic political novel *Odd Man Out*, again about a loner being pursued by outside forces. In his novel of *On the Night of the Fire,* the geographical location is fictitious, it is a place called Punter Ward and the street names (chiefly Kepnor Street), are duplicated in the film. Green grew up in Portsmouth and lived in Belfast, he may have suggested Newcastle as a possible location as there was a direct train line from London, which would reduce transport costs.

The film production crew is in fact a *Who's Who* of film making. The cameraman was the German emigre, Gunter Krampf, who clearly brought to bear the Expressionist influence of his native country's cinema. With his lenses, Newcastle's scenes became dark, shadowy sets reflecting the emotional tension and suspense of the story. The screenplay was by a young Terence Fisher. Fisher was influenced by the French cinema trend known as poetic realism, mainly under director Marcel Carne. These 1930s' French films were set in working class suburbs - and significantly in ports and shipyards, which again may have influenced the choice of Newcastle. Fisher was destined to become the director of James Bond films. The film editor was Terence Young. He used his slightly static approach to editing this atmospheric film in later years as the director of many Hammer films. A sequence where the camera suddenly focusses on the ever paranoid Kobling sharpening his razor is pure Hitchcock, while the fire scenes and the crowd effects are not unlike the Fritz Lang classic *Fury*.

Intriguingly, the reason why Newcastle was chosen as a location may remain a mystery and director Hurst's autobiography remains unpublished.

Named or unnamed, Newcastle is the main protagonist in what is probably the earliest example of British Film Noir, where a small act has dark and fatal consequences. One cannot help but have sympathy for Will Kobling, a well-intentioned man trapped by fate.

Ralph Richardson pitches his performance perfectly. It is the first of a line of cinematic lineage that includes *Gaslight* and *The Third Man*.

On the Night of the Fire caught local press attention in 1939. The *Evening Chronicle* proclaimed 'MURDER FILM SHOT IN NEWCASTLE!' It premiered on June 24th 1940 at the Queen's and Pavilion cinemas. Unfortunately, local critics considered it to be too grim a story for wartime audiences who ultimately sought escape from the darkness of the reality facing them.

The *Chronicle* critic wrote '*As general entertainment in the dark days of war it is in my opinion a dismal failure*'. Time would tell and it has been critically re-assessed and praised here and in the USA. It remains currently unavailable for commercial release.

And there are still long shadows falling on Dog Leap Stairs...........

MURDER FILM SHOT IN NEWCASTLE

Stars Mingle With Quayside Crowds

By FRANK EVANS

NEWCASTLE has been turned this week-end into a film studio. Such famous players as Ralph Richardson, Diana Wynyard, Romney Brent, Mary Clare and Sara Allgood have been making scenes in the heart of the city for a new film called, "On the Night of the Fire."

Most of the story—which is one of theft leading to blackmail and murder—has been played in The Close, near Forth Banks.

Ralph Richardson has had a scene on the Tyne Bridge. He and Diana Wynyard have been shot moving crowds in the ......

.... for their ......

........, who began his screen career as assistant to Ford on "The Informer," is thrilled by the locations he has found. "Newcastle," he says, "is the most filmic city I have ever been in. Why hasn't it been used before? All those bridges ....

The Clouded Yellow (1951)

Trevor Howard as David Summers
Jean Simmons as Sophie Malreaux
Maxwell Reed as Hick
Barry Jones as Nicholas Fenton
Sonia Dresdel as Jess Fenton
Kenneth More as Willy Shipley
Directed by Ralph Thomas
Produced by Betty Box

The city of Newcastle was totally uncredited in *On the Night of the Fire* in 1939, but in 1951 its 'sombre dignity' earned it a vital cameo role in the espionage thriller *The Clouded Yellow*.

The film's title relates to a breed of butterfly - part of a collection owned by the mysterious couple Nicholas and Jess Fenton. The intricate work of cataloguing falls to David Somers (Trevor Howard), who always sported a cravat as stylishly as Leslie Phillips.

Somers is a burnt-out MI5 agent seeking recuperation and possibly retirement in the Fenton's apparently idyllic rural surroundings. He befriends a seemingly disturbed young woman, Sophie (Jean Simmons) who is the Fenton's over-protected niece. Sophie is suddenly accused of the murder of Hick (Maxwell Reed), the lecherous and cocky local gardener and handyman. David and Sophie suddenly find themselves on the run from both the police and Somers' MI5 colleague Willy Shipley (Kenneth More).

Their flight to prove her innocence first takes them to Newcastle where Somers has a safe house owned by the Cesares family who, in his previous career, he saved from the Nazis. The Cesares occupy a house easily identified as Burdon Terrace in Jesmond - a perfect suburban front to hide their identities behind lush foliage and bay windows. The fugitives catch a bus to the Town Moor area of Gosforth as the Cesares watch them from the Haymarket bus station, Central Station and St Nicholas's Cathedral area. Following a glimpse of Princess Mary Maternity Hospital there is a powerful atmosphere of Film Noir as they travel by boat from the murkiness of the Long Stairs on the Quayside.

From Newcastle, with Kenneth More and the authorities in hot pursuit, the duo go on to hide in the stunningly filmed Lake District and then a chaotic dockside Liverpool. The real villain is revealed at the now demolished Liverpool Overhead Railway and Sophie is vindicated thanks to Somers' wartime skills which include getting her hair cut to tomboy length for disguise.

Throughout the film the urbane Howard and the enigmatic, wide-eyed Simmons (prior to her Hollywood stardom) make for an alluring, if odd and tense couple. Is she disturbed after all? We can only speculate.

The Clouded Yellow is another touchstone production in the history of post-war British film. It was co-written by espionage master Eric Ambler and writer Janet Green. Green would go on to script another important North East film *A Life For Ruth* filmed in Seaham harbour and the ground-breaking gay-issue film *Victim*. *The Clouded Yellow* was the first production for the legendary Betty Box - she re-mortgaged her house to finance it.

Director Ralph Thomas would direct thirty-two films with Box, including the incredibly successful *Doctor* series. *The Clouded Yellow* was Box's first independent film.

Newcastle has a perfectly formed role in a film Alfred Hitchcock would be proud of. Box and Thomas give us a typical Hitchcock theme of the falsely accused on the run in a world of paranoia and betrayal. If you're thinking *The Thirty-Nine Steps*, it's no co-incidence that Ralph Thomas would go on to steer his own version of the Buchan classic starring two cast members from *The Clouded Yellow* - crafty old Barry Evans [a missing finger?] and the affable Kenneth More as a quixotic Richard Hannay.

The Clouded Yellow highlights a post-war obsession with espionage and the adverse effects on the psychology of damaged agents like David Somers. You can throw in a touch of *The Third Man* as the Newcastle waterside and suburbs rival the secrets held in old Vienna.

Ultimately, *The Clouded Yellow,* even in Hitchcock's incredible hands, could have been restricted by studio-bound sets of moorlands, urban and suburban locations, instead the choice of stunning exteriors and the unprecedented decision to film on location gives Newcastle pride of place in what I still think is an under-rated British classic.

Two tickets to Jesmond please!

JEAN SIMMONS
TREVOR HOWARD
SONIA DRESDEL in

J. Arthur Rank Organisation presents

THE CLOUDED YELLOW

with BARRY JONES and MAXWELL REED

Screenplay by Jane Green
Produced by Betty E. Box
Directed by Ralph Thomas
A BETTY E. BOX Independent Production for Carillon Films.

EAGLE-LION DISTRIBUTION

PRINTED IN ENGLAND

Payroll (1961)

Michael Craig as Johnny Mellor
Billlie Whitelaw as Jackie Parker
Francois Prevost as Katie Pearson
William Lucas as Dennis Pearson
Kenneth Griffith as Monty
Tom Bell as Blackie
Directed by Sidney Hayers
Music by Reg Owen

We've seen Newcastle suffer screen anonymity in 1939, get a good cameo in 1951…now for its grand entrance!

As *Payroll* opens, the big screen fills with a big thanks from the producers to the City of Newcastle upon Tyne!

In the *Evening Chronicle* on August 15th 1960, the film's director, Sidney Hayers, proclaimed: 'We were fascinated by the high and low levels of the city, which have interesting dramatic possibilities'

As with any movie in Britain in the 60s, *Payroll* reflects the culture of the times. From the late 1950s, in a post-imperial, war-wearied Britain, the working class were on the march in literature, on stage and then onto the screen. John Osborne's Jimmy Porter looked back in anger - we will meet Osborne himself in a future Newcastle-based movie. John Braine's Joe Lampton defied the taboos of sex and class to make his own *Room at the Top* and Arthur Seaton from *Saturday Night and Sunday Morning* cried 'Don't let the bastards grind you down'. A new wave of British filmmakers was filming in the North - on location in Leeds, Manchester, Huddersfield, Liverpool. The films were mainly black and white with natural lighting - a lot of rain fell on industrial landscapes and broken buildings - giving us a new freedom of expression.

The British crime movie mirrored this revolution, often embodied by actors like Stanley Baker, who portrayed detectives or gangsters with equal hardness. His quest for justice took no prisoners as he chased villains across Manchester rooftops in the 1959 *Hell is a City*. Invariably there was a Brit Jazz soundtrack.

In the real 60s' Britain crime rose at an alarming rate during the decade. Gone were the post-war spiv-racketeers and racecourse touts, as materialism and working class affluence drove men to bond on a one-off basis to steal money with violence and then escape with the spoils. This was known as 'project' crime and it is where, in 1961, *Payroll* comes in.

Payroll is a classic heist movie set in a Newcastle before T. Dan Smith's wrecking ball created a new vision of the city. Michael Craig (like an early version of Clive Owen) is a slick, ruthless leader of a gang, two members of which are played by veteran British character actors - Tom Bell is the psychopathically impatient Blackie and Kenneth Griffith plays the weak, self-doubting Monty.

These desperate men meticulously plan to ambush and rob a factory payroll car. We see them observing and timing the van as it leaves Lloyds Bank in Grey Street and travels to its factory destination via Dean Street. Their best laid plans go awry when the company increases their vigilance by using an armoured car, manned by two security men. Now the gang will have to deploy ram-raiding tactics - blocking the van en route to the factory and jamming police radio signals.

Their inside information comes from a desperate accountant called Pearson, cuckolded financially by his French-accented wife (played by Francois Prevost who seems to have wandered in from another film noir). She develops a fatal attraction to the criminal Johnny Mellor as her husband crumbles under pressure. She is motivated by money and greed, feeling that their materialism gets a poor return living as they do in a Tynemouth house, around the corner from the Tynemouth Plaza on the seafront. She consummates her passion with Mellor in the dunes by Seaton Sluice.

The heist itself is filmed with forensic realism. The innocent 60s audience must have felt that the ram-raid on the Tyne Bridge was extremely violent. The armoured car guard fatally shoots a gang member, and the driver, carrying his child's teddy bear, is killed when the trucks collide. His raincoat-wearing wife, Jackie, portrayed by Billie Whitelaw, is revenge on two legs. She will eventually by-pass the police to exact her own justice.

After the heist, events unravel like a Shakesperian tragedy. One gang member spills the beans when intoxicated in what must be the only Newcastle pub totally frequented by cockneys. Later, in a stunning scene, filmed beneath a benighted High Level Bridge, his body is disposed of - or is it? There is a classic double-cross finale, a death by quicksand and that *The Third Man* feeling again as Billy Whitelaw pursues her quarry down the Long Stairs. The film makes maximum use of crumbling lockups near the Chapman Electrical Factors chateau-style building near Central Station. The gang's hide-out is opposite The Cooperage.

With the magic of cinema, scenes are intercut with locations in Surrey and Rugby. The whole thing paces along with a jazz score by Reg Owen combining a feel of *Peter Gunn* and Dankworth's *Avengers* Theme.

Sidney Hayers directs without wasting a shot or word of script and the film is an exercise in being lean and mean. He would go on to direct horror classics such as *Night of the Eagle* before disappearing into the jungle of American television drama. Billie Whitelaw and Tom Bell would ironically reappear together in the Kray brother's movie. Manchester may have gone under the film title *Hell is a City*, but it could have easily applied to Newcastle.

Right: *Newcastle as 'Heist City'.*

The Likely Lads (1964-66)
Whatever Happened to the Likely Lads (1973-74)
The Likely Lads (Feature Film) (1976)

Dick Clement and Ian La Frenais launched *The Likely Lads* in 1964, unwittingly based on a sketch *Double Date* that Clement, an Essex born BBC trainee director, had co-written with Tynemouth-born market researcher Ian La Frenais. For decades they created hugely successful TV series of dramas infused with comedy and acute conversational observation of the human condition. Now based in Beverley Hills, the duo have articulated the working classes in factories, offices, pubs, prisons and building sites - paralleled with a movie-writing career. Newcastle and the Geordie attitude to life have not been far away from their sights.

Between 1964 and 1966 *The Likely Lads* introduced us to Bob Ferris and Terry Collier, young working class men at work and play in a post-war North East - or what is inferred to be the North East. Their exploits are not seen as a string of sight gags but as crafted comedy mini-dramas, as they attempt to score with the opposite sex, go on holiday, buy a scooter as a first mode of transport, sample free love and attempt to emigrate or join the army, all of which enthralled a nation of viewers.

We not only witness Bob and Terry's scrapes and their encounters in dance halls, workshops, offices and restaurants, we more significantly witness their hilarious and perceptive discussions about their working class lot in life. These discussions invariably take place in the pub. Bob and Terry epitomise a newly mobile generation in a grey post-war Britain. They begin to question old values and more importantly have a disposable income that can be spent on football, meals, booze, birds and travel, once the rent has been paid.

Thanks to the acute joint observations of Clement and La Frenais *The Likely Lads* was pivotal in the broadcasting emancipation of the North East. The region and the city of Newcastle were blatantly used as locations from the 1930s to the 1960s but they were never referenced and there was never a local

Right: Fishing with the Likely Lads near Haughton Castle, 1973.

accent heard. The BBC Home Service had patronised the area with a few local programmes but the only regional accent that the nation was attuned to was that of Lancashire and Yorkshire, the conveyor of national variety and humour through the likes of George Formby and Gracie Fields.

Rodney Bewes and James Bolam were respectively from Yorkshire and Sunderland, so perhaps it is ironic that they are credited with launching the Geordie accent on an unsuspecting audience. BBC audience surveys of the launch of *The Likely Lads* even contained audience comments that the lads were tearaway Midlanders! Equally ironic was that the original series was filmed in Willesden, a London suburb, and on a location trip to Norfolk. The early series of *The Likely Lads* imply rather than directly reference the North East. The lads' workplace seems to be an electrical factory possibly near Hartlepool or could it be Newcastle?

The series was a product of the British New Wave of drama, theatre, cinema and music. Ian La Frenais told me, 'We were both late gatecrashers to this party but we got in.' Bewes and Bolam had both been in British New Wave films prior to television. *Coronation Street* (not initially shown on Tyne Tees) and *Z Cars* (an inspiration to Clement and La Frenais) had projected a working class sensibility of the North onto our screens but not a North Eastern one. Alan Plater, when writing for *Z Cars*, faced great opposition when the Tyne Dock born actor, John Woodvine, wanted to play a visiting inspector in character as a Geordie! Thanks to *The Likely Lads* the North East was at last on the screen and on the scene and crossing over into millions of homes. At last the TV opened the floodgates for Geordie actors.

Before The Likely Lads *and* When the Boat Comes In *there were no Geordie actors on screen - after them they were crawling all over it!*

Ian La Frenais

My favourite episode of *The Likely Lads* (very few episodes survive today) is *The Other Side of the Fence*. It is a humorous and sad look at class distinction in the workplace. Bob is seconded into a white-collar job in the factory office and scorned by the salesmen. He takes Terry to a work's office dance only to be told that Terry, being from the factory floor, is not eligible and asked to leave. In support, Bob tells his boss to stick the job and his forthcoming promotion. This defence of class discrimination is a theme that will recur between the lads when they return in the 70s. It is a perfect example of giving national political issues a workplace exposure in a regional setting.

When it was launched in 1964, the *Radio Times* referred to Ian La Frenais as 'a Northerner' and used the title *The Likely Lads* as a comment on lively (potentially good or bad) young men, as observed by older Northern male onlookers chewing tobacco! (It's also a boxing term which may have some relevance). Either way, Bob and Terry don't miss much and are touted by BBC publicity as 'acquisitive, irreverent - at their age they're idealists - but injected with a strong shot of common sense'

*

Whatever Happened to the Likely Lads (1973-74) reunites Bob and Terry in a new decade. The lads are back, this time in colour and on location in Newcastle and the surrounding region. This is a very different context for both of them. Terry has served in the armed forces and had an unsuccessful marriage. His return to the North East reveals a changed social, physical and political landscape. Bob, who was supposed to join the army but was discharged for having flat feet, is now upwardly mobile. He is marrying lower middle-class librarian Thelma, whose father is a successful, self-made builder. Bob and Thelma are ecstatic at moving into their new-build house on the Elm Lodge Estate (actual location Killingworth). Thelma is naturally suspicious of the returning Terry's influence on her future husband. The comic tensions of the series are illustrated by the fact that Terry's past is being bulldozed along with the slum clearances, and Bob's bright future is being newly built. This is reflected in the opening and closing credits of the series. We see Commercial Road in Byker, Cruddas Park flats, which were the showpiece of T. Dan Smith's rejuvenation scheme, and the cranes and derelict chimney of Ouseburn. The demolition theme continues with a view of Todd's Nook flats through piles of bricks and fallen masonry on Gloucester Road.

When Terry comes home from the army after five years he faces 70s' consumerism - it's all Blue Nun, fondues and flared trousers - the life he knew has been bulldozed away forever. He had no career.

Ian La Frenais

One of the most poignant episodes is entitled *Moving On*. Bob and Terry revisit the haunts of their misspent youth, when you didn't have to take anything seriously until after you were twenty-five. Terry finds all his dream palaces are rubble or new buildings - The Go-Go Club has gone, and it is now Gateshead's *Get Carter* car park! In an incredible aerial shot from that car park the lads reflect on their past and future. The Roxy Ballroom is now Newcastle Civic Centre - 'All my memories were there!'

Their favourite coffee bar is now the Cruddas Park shopping centre. The Saturday morning picture house is demolished and only Eric's fish and chip shop survives. 'I am being bulldozed,' says Terry. The *Whatever Happened to the Likely Lads* series capitalised on the tension between staying in the past where we were safe in a community of terraced housing or moving into a modern high-rise and housing estate future. Terry is a reactionary and anti-progress, avoiding life's responsibilities. He uses nostalgia and a rose-tinted illusion of their collective past to trap and tempt Bob away from a lifestyle of identical driveways, badminton and brown and orange colour schemes. Bob it seems, mainly because of Thelma, wants to embrace this new ideal away from working class roots, but it is not to be achieved without a fight from Terry Collier, coupled with his own often pathological self-doubt. Terry's reactionary attitude is summarised in the episode *No Hiding Place*. He finds that a barber he used to frequent has become a unisex hairdresser. He confides in Bob, who is totally at home with hair conditioner and coiffeurs, that the male assistants, who seem to be holding him at ransom in the chair, may have alternative sexual proclivities. This misreading of cultural change has a lineage that leads straight up to Peter Kay's 'garlic bread' routine.

The Likely Lads avoid the 70s reality of power cuts, refuse strikes and glam rock. Bob warns Terry that he is destined to be a loner - 'The Shane of Elm Lodge Estate,' because Terry is so scornful of its soulless domestic cloning. The series denouement is strategically left open to interpretation. Terry is confronted by reality when a close relation dies with a reputation of being as feckless and irresponsible as himself. Maybe at last Terry has seen the writing on the wall - or has he? Bob and Thelma walk into the suburban sunset and curiously in the last episode into a wife-swapping scenario!

Our last ever encounter with Bob and Terry is courtesy of the 1976 feature film *The Likely Lads*. Making the transition from TV sitcom to the big screen can be a recipe for disaster, although one of the great success stories of this genre was Hammer Films version of *On the Buses*!

Once again Clement and La Frenais, as with their cinema version of *Porridge*, succeeded with *The Likely Lads* feature. When interviewing Ian La Frenais I have always sensed however, that they weren't totally happy with the results:

The film has some good moments and I love the Tynemouth fishing location sequence towards the end. It was just that we couldn't leave the USA during production, so we couldn't be as hands on as we might have been - we didn't want it to be just another 'telly film' besides it didn't have a big enough budget.

Ian La Frenais

The plot is a game of two halves, once again looking at the social and cultural pressures faced through the two lads' outlook on life.

Terry may be settling down and is holding down a job of sorts in sales. He has been rehoused in a decaying block of flats where courting couples inhabit the lifts and Bob's car is vandalised when he visits. This is an interesting echo of T. Dan Smith's high rise dreams going sour. Bob's middle class pretensions, boosted by Thelma, cause him to scoff at Terry's new lifestyle.

Bob: *Soulless concrete blocks!*
Terry: *What do you mean? It's got a modern kitchen, a lovely view, and an inside lavatory.*
Bob: *These things (the terraced housing of their childhood) had poetry.*
Terry: *There's not much poetry at four in the morning padding down the yard to a freezing outside bog.*

from Don't Look Now: British Cinema in the 1970s

Terry's new relationship allows Thelma to hope that his threat to their marital bliss will diffuse. The two couples set off on a disastrous caravan holiday. In a classic scene Thelma and Terry's girlfriend are stranded in their dressing gowns in front of a vicar and congregation at Corbridge church. This is followed by a mid-life crisis for Bob Ferris and the two boys attempt to recapture their reckless youth in a Whitley Bay boarding house. Thelma and Bob eventually reunite and Terry once more ducks out to join the merchant navy. There is of course a twist as Bob heads for Bahrain against his will.

The film was very well received in the North East and is still regarded with great affection forty years on. This is partly due to the readily identified locations. A view of the Tyne Bridge from City Road and Tarsett Street frames Bob and Terry as they kick a football with local lads and witness the demolition of their favourite pub The Fat Ox. Bob clutches the dart board to his chest as a symbol of all that was dear to him, nostalgia being a vital thread in *The Likely Lads*. We see them on Wallsend High Street and Atkinson Street and Whitley Bay seafront. Terry's flat is part of the now demolished flats in Howdon. Ian La Frenais' favourite shot is of Terry Collier fishing on Tynemouth pier, a scene that was actually filmed in sub-zero conditions. The Newcastle of this film is not far removed from the bleakness of *Get Carter*. A number of authors have made the point that our final glimpses of Bob and Terry are as figures dwarfed by the local landscape of docks, cranes and slum clearance.

Bolam and Bewes would never reunite and only Ant and Dec paid a brief homage in a sketch revival on ITV in 2002.

There is something harsher about the Lads too - deprived of the warmth of the studio interiors and TV's head-and-shoulder shots of Bob and Terry together at the pub, they become figures in a ruined landscape. Bob's mid-life crisis makes him bitter and spiteful, while Terry's faults shine even brighter. It's not quite Carter's world but it is one he would recognise.

from *The Likely Lads* by Phil Wickham

NCJ MEDIA

ARRON CUPID/WHITLEY BAY FILM FESTIVAL

Top: *'Honest man Bob, it was this big'.*
Above: *Author Chris Phipps interviews Ian La Frenais at the Whitley Bay Film Festival.*

Dont Look Back (1967)

Directed by D.A. Pennebaker

Newcastle City Hall is a venue beloved of performers ranging from Kathleen Ferrier to Bruce Springsteen to AC/DC.

Hank B Marvin recalled to me about seeing the American Blues legend Big Bill Broonzy there in the 50s, and Bryan Ferry remembered watching Chris Barber and Ottilie Paterson blasting out trad jazz to his youthful ears.

The City Hall has had silver screen appearances - most recently in the bittersweet 'pensioner joins a choir' opus *A Song for Marion* starring Vanessa Redgrave and Terence Stamp, filmed in 2012.

Its greatest role is in D.A. Pennebaker's ground-breaking documentary *Dont Look Back*, an intimate pioneering 'fly on the wall' look at Bob Dylan's 1965 UK tour. Dylan is charismatic and growing in self-confidence as he arrives at Newcastle City Hall - on hand is Alan Price, who had recently quit The Animals.

Tyneside Musicologist Rob Byron comments:

When Bob Dylan walked onstage at Newcastle City Hall on Thursday 6 May 1965 he was not the worldwide superstar he would be a little over twelve months later when he would return to the city, this time to play the Odeon. True, he'd scored a Top Ten hit with his first UK single release *The times they are a-changin'* the previous month but it's fair to say that he was a cult artist, albeit one gathering considerable pace.

He was between what are regarded as two of his finest albums. *Bringing it all back Home* had just been released some six weeks earlier and *Highway 61 Revisited* would be recorded upon his return to the US in June and released in August.

The event that was to catapult Dylan to global recognition was the recording of his *Mr Tambourine Man* by a then little-known bunch of Beatles freaks formed in Los Angeles called The Byrds. The Byrds version had been released in the US in April (May in UK) and would top the charts on both sides of the pond on July 24 - a rare feat in those days.

Another Dylan cover *All I really wanna do* would go top five the following month for the band. Meanwhile back in the US, on June 16, Dylan recorded *Like a Rolling Stone*. A truly ground-breaking six-minute song that would change the face of popular music forever.

In the movie shot on the seven city UK concert tour, there is some wonderful concert footage shot both onstage and backstage, and indeed some shot in Newcastle City Centre.

In the movie Dylan is seen standing outside a store selling guitars. This is Jeavons in Pudding Chare, just off the Bigg Market. They sold musical instruments, also sheet music and records. They would always advertise new releases by using a form of easily removable whitewash and in the movie you can clearly see Dylan's new release *Subterranean Homesick Blues* advertised in this way - just above is the latest release by Cilla Black. But Dylan is transfixed by the guitars 'They don't have those guitars in the States, man. They're incredible. Twenty grand?' The guitars are actually priced up in guineas, an old pre-decimal pricing method (A guinea equated to £1 and 1 shilling) but for some reason Dylan appears to think they're £20,000. Incidentally, just for the record, this guitar shop incident has been erroneously listed on YouTube as having occurred in London and/or Liverpool but it is neither, it is definitely Newcastle upon Tyne. The premises are now occupied by a pizza restaurant. Although not shown in the original film, Dylan is filmed trying on and buying a new jacket and tie at the then very trendy Marcus Price store in the Groat Market, just around the corner from the guitar store. This footage is available as extras in the 2006 box set.

Dylan is filmed arriving at the City Hall stage door in College Street to a gaggle of excited Geordie lads & lasses. It's difficult to imagine him understanding what they were saying as he'd had trouble with Alan Price's accent elsewhere in the movie.

Backstage at Newcastle City Hall, Bob is shown playing the piano with his producer Tom Wilson at his side. He is then seen arguing with a well-dressed, well spoken, preppie looking student type. It materialises he is a Science student, which Dylan seems to find highly amusing, and it would appear he is interviewing Dylan for his student magazine. All the time Dylan is tuning his guitar and pacing the dressing room. The Science student, who takes some stick from 'His Bobness', is in fact Terry Ellis who went on to co-found Chrysalis Records and manage Jethro Tull.

This interview is interrupted with a message that the High Sherriff of Newcastle would like to meet Bob. This is Theresa Russell who at the time was the Lord Mayor in waiting. Dylan is reluctant to see her; his people say she's a big cheese. 'Who is she?', he asks. He's still hesitant but obviously relents as in the next frame we see him listening intently to this gracious lady. She introduces her three sons and tells Bob that if he should return next May he could stay with her family in the Mansion House (the official residence of the Lord Mayor of Newcastle - he did return but didn't stay there). Dylan is very respectful of this lady and she is presented with a harmonica, the same one that the Science student had just previously refused, on account of the fact that he 'couldn't play it'.

Once the dressing room is cleared of guests. Alan Price, the Animals recently departed keyboard player is seen playing a jaunty version of George Formby's *Leaning on a Lampost*, then Dave Berry's *Little Things*, after which Dylan questions him on why he's no longer with the band.... 'it just happens you know'. The scene in the backstage dressing room finishes with the now infamous footage of Alan Price opening a bottle of Newcastle Brown Ale on the edge of the piano.

Dylan is then shown onstage performing a snippet of *Don't think twice, it's alright*.

An almost full version of *It Ain't Me Babe* is available on the aforementioned extras disc, interspersed with footage of Dylan's departure from Newcastle Central Station the following day, followed by a dozen or so fans who run along with the train as it departs for Manchester.

'I hope this train can out run those kids' says Dylan.

'I'd like to see them try that at Grand Central' quips his side-kick and foil Bob Neuwirth.

Stills from the film *Dont Look Back*
Top: *Dylan on Pudding Chare admiring the guitars in Jeavons window.*
Right: *Dylan tries on a tie in Marcus Price watched by his manager Albert Grossman and Alan Price - both drinking Newcastle Brown Ale.*

STILLS FROM DONT LOOK BACK BY DA PENNEBAKER
COURTESY PENNEBAKER HEGEDUS FILMS AND ASHES & SAND INC.

A Turn Up for Tony (1968)

Tyne Tees Television, 29 minutes featuring Tony Tanner and Ted Lune.

Now available on the British Film Institute website, this silent comedy short was shot on Tyneside in 1968 and reflects, perhaps unwittingly, some of T. Dan Smith's changes to the city.

Tony, played by distinguished Broadway and West End actor Tony Tanner, is a daydreaming, unemployed Geordie workman.

We follow his Walter Mitty style escapades as he pursues a woman working at a cigarette kiosk in Pink Lane, between what was then Lindano's restaurant and the Wine Bar opposite.

Tony has the appearance of Andy Capp, clothed in cap and muffler. Throughout the story he is pursued by a comic tramp played by music hall veteran Ted Lune. Leaving the Salvation Army Hostel in Dog Bank, Tony, in the most stunning shot of the film, crosses a huge demolition site to contemplate the newly constructed Cruddas Park flats on Scotswood Road. In a single pan the story of the transition between old and new is told. The other interesting sequence involves Tony finding himself as a James Bond figure in the casino of the Dolce Vita Club. This venue was linked to the infamous one-arm bandit murders and inspired one of the main storylines in *Get Carter* three years later. Its use in this plot is darkly comic. In the front entrance Tommy Cooper and Jonnie Ray are advertised as coming attractions.

I won't issue a spoiler alert - just watch this delightful Keatonesque film on the BFI site.

Cruddas Park flats in Elswick, regular stars of north-east film and TV.

Amber Films (1968-)

Graeme Rigby from Amber once told me, 'If people say don't go over there into that corner - I think Amber should'

Amber Film and Photography Collective formed in London in 1968 and moved to the North East in 1969. Since then, in moving and still images, they have captured the marginal lives and livings of the North East. Without Amber most of this material and social documentation would be ignored, undervalued and lost. Mining, fishing, harness-racing and many other communities are not shown in a patronising or cold way in the productions, in fact they become directly involved and evolve with Amber's community approach. The results are stunning (and often controversial) dramas, documentaries and docu-dramas.

Their first production *Maybe* (1969) captured the reflections on life of an engine man on the Shields Ferry. It is alleged that the BBC would not show it due to what it considered indecipherable dialect. Amber remained undeterred. This film and Tom Hadaway's fishing industry drama *The Filleting Machine* had a formative effect on actress Charlie Hardwick:

I would go as far to say that Amber Films or at least *The Filleting Machine* was the first thing about the north I had ever seen on the TV (apart from *Kes)* when I was a girl. It really captivated my imagination. I didn't know you could have working class characters and working class actors and subjects as hard hitting and as passionate as Tom Hadaway's little piece - he was in it himself with Amber Styles. When I saw it I think that consolidated something in me that said 'you could be involved in this!'

I joined Wallsend Youth Theatre while I was a civil servant working at the Ministry. The youth theatre was the bridge between the two worlds and seeing *The Filleting Machine* blew my mind because of its authenticity, its passion, its anger, it was about working class people, it was about people that I had met and was a bit scared of. I had never seen those ideas and those passions on film before. I didn't know you could be an actor if you had a Geordie accent!

It was not until *The Likely Lads* and Amber before the North East dialect became acceptable in the wider field. I still go for auditions and people say 'I'm sorry but where are you from?' We were a group of young actors starting at the youth theatre and at the Live Theatre (which was connected to Amber Films). It was woven from politics, the arts and passion about our region and its people. Those that weren't normally represented *actually* got represented. Amber gave the voice to the voiceless! Or gave a voice to those that aren't heard.

Some people have said 'If Amber turn up it usually means that things are going to get demolished!' Part of their remit was to document working class life in the North East, through photography, through documentary and feature films, and they have done precisely what they set out to do. What is in their archive would have been blown away on the wind across the sea and that would be the end of it. But it's there, documented from the fella on the ferry going across the Tyne between the yards, to the miners' wives of Easington that featured in *The Scar*.

The Scar was a heck of a role for me, I believed passionately in the cause in the first place and we were active in the Miners' strike.

Charlie Hardwick

The Scar became a milestone in Charlie's acting career. A portrait of an estranged miner's wife, she is disillusioned and shattered by the political betrayal of the miners' strike outcome. She finds herself compromised by starting a relationship with the manager of an opencast mine in the area. It reflected Hardwick's real life political dedication.

Amber was directly instrumental in preserving Newcastle's Quayside area where they are now based. A key film in the multimedia (and ultimately successful) campaign to get Quayside buildings listed and saved from the wrecking ball was 1979's *Quayside*:

Quayside (1979)

Directed by Peter Roberts and Murray Martin

Quayside is described as a poetic portrait of Newcastle's Quayside area. Watching it you feel almost like an intruder into a vanishing world. The few people you see or just glimpse as the camera moves seem ghost-like. There are landmarks like the wonderfully named Old Tunis Cafe, the Quayside news agency resplendent with adverts for Castella and Capstan, the cobbles of Hanover Street and narrow roads passing bonded warehouses and a skeletal gasometer. They are all here, a dog (literally) on Dog Leap Stairs, the Baltic Mills, and the wedge of Phoenix House at the bottom of Dean Street. Then there is of course the river with its murky waters captured in dream-like camera swoops under the iron and brick archways of the great bridges. The most stunning shot is a backwards pan and track of the incline of Dean Street. We could almost be on the set of Nevil Shute's *On the Beach*.

As with many Amber films, there is no traditional narration or commentary, you have to join up the dots for yourself. The images combine with snatches of dialogue as disembodied voices relate memoirs of the power of the thirty-six local ship companies, the many job possibilities and the vanished prosperity of the area. This is a technique redolent of the Charles Parker's BBC *Radio Ballads*. Ship horns blow and the *Bessie Surtees* passes under the Swing Bridge. There is a plaintive harmonica which plays *Wooden Heart*. The concluding comment off-screen is 'All of Tyneside is a mess.' You cannot disagree - and for once the building preservation pundits actually watched, listened and acted.

Murray Martin (a founder member of Amber) persuaded the council to add many of the Quayside's buildings to the Listed Buildings Register. So where Amber are now based, and buildings like Malmaison - right the way along the Quayside, wouldn't exist - but thanks to him it's still here.

Charlie Hardwick

T. Dan Smith seems to haunt the pages of this book. His high-rise creations dominate dramas and documentaries as does Smith himself. He is thinly disguised as Austin Donohue in *Our Friends in the North*, but now he actually appears as himself in Amber's ambitious noirish pastiche:

T Dan Smith:
A Funny thing happened on the way to Utopia
(1987)

Written, Directed and Produced by Amber

Amber filmmakers Steve Trafford and Murray Martin appear as journalists investigating the possible civic and national political goings-on surrounding T. Dan Smith. As related elsewhere in this book, Smith was a controversial city council leader, jailed for alleged corruption in 1974 for involvement with the builder/architect John Poulson. It was alleged that Smith, in a PR role, had received bribes for ensuring high rise building contracts conveniently went Poulson's way. So the question is - was Smith a visionary or a villain - or both?

This is a demanding film as it interweaves fact and fiction. It has a master card to play - Smith himself collaborated with the makers and actually appears in it. This is before he agreed to be part subject of Peter Flannery's *Our Friends in the North*.

There seem to be at least two parallel plot strands. Factually, the film makers/journalists interview Smith, view existing news archive, including BBC's *Dan's Castle*, in an effort to put new light onto the civic and ministerial cover-ups involved in Smith's eventual incarceration.

This investigation interweaves a fictional plot which is a dramatisation/parody of the actual events. Smith and Poulson are respectively transposed into the fictional councillor Alan Deal and builder Jack Cross. This story of bribery and high rise building contracts threatens to bring everybody down and a local newsreader announces 'Councillor accepts bribes. Five million pounds paid to Cross Construction.' Of course those higher up the political chain remain immune, sipping sherry in the Metropolis, saying in their defence 'All I ever sold Jack Cross was good advice.'

The film has an air of a political thriller. Trafford and Martin are like a low-fi versions of *All the President's Men* as they sift through newsreels in their edit suite, consume fish and chips, and sink pints in Quayside taverns. There are definite noir touches too - Smith's limousine glides through the night, shadows are thrown under bridges and archways, and the investigators walk through underpasses and even the halls of government. Once again there is the solitary harmonica courtesy of Ray Stubbs. One of the most uncomfortable scenes, filmed in St Cuthbert's Village, is a confrontation between high rise tenants and Jack Cross, accompanied by their Tory MP.

T. Dan Smith of course talks of his lifelong Trotskyism and his possible MI5 profile and he remains articulate yet ambiguous in all things. In reply to the question, 'Were you corrupted by the power structure?' he replies 'I had access, but I fought the corner of the provinces, of the poor and the running down of industry.'

This film is a fascinating puzzle, like the noir classic *The Big Sleep*, it is a great watch but is ultimately unsolvable.

Of *Quayside* and *T. Dan Smith*, *Billy Elliot* writer, Lee Hall says:

Amber and the Side Gallery have been hugely inspirational for my work. Live Theatre (where I have produced many of my plays) and Amber emerged from the same cultural moment. The need for a new generation whose outlook had been formed by the cultural shifts in the 1960s to record the lives of working class communities was very urgent. A whole load of people, often themselves from working class backgrounds had gone to college and become very interested in the Arts but found the places they came from were not properly represented. Amber's mission to use the tradition of documentary photography and to expand this into film was one of the most extraordinary cultural achievements in post-war Britain.

What they managed to record, of course, was the collapse of a whole way of life and the destruction of the geography in which it took place. Newcastle in the Sixties was still largely defined by the heavy industry which had been the engine of its prosperity. It created large urban areas where working class people lived and that way of life was culturally very strong. Of course the past fifty years has seen profound economic changes which have changed these areas profoundly. To be quite honest I didn't see the Amber films until I was an adult but knew the photography very well. My grandparents were from Byker so it was all very familiar. But what all their films did was to record something that was vanishing before our eyes. It's fundamentally what film does at its core anyway; captures a moment of time which would be lost without that 'witnessing'. But what makes Amber's films have a unique resonance is the fact they were recording a much greater disappearance. That they were alert to our ideas of politics passing as much as the social losses is credit to their alertness about these profound shifts. T. Dan Smith is a pivotal figure in this story and, of course, a pivotal figure in the landscape of the City. He is absolutely instrumental in starting the boom in Arts in the region. He understood the importance of the Arts both culturally and economically for ordinary working class people in the City and his thinking influenced everything that's happened since.

He, like Amber, was alert to artistic and cultural movements across Europe, and beyond, and saw that Newcastle should be a part of that. However, where Amber were alert to what was being lost in this attempt to modernise the City, Smith was a strong promulgator of the Sixties Modernism which would transform the City. There is a strange tension between the older generation of Socialists who had a vision of central planning and love of Modern Architecture to ameliorate social ills and the younger generation who saw beauty in the grime that Smith was trying to sweep away. These two films really capture this conflict. There is a melancholy in both of these films. Both Smith and the ordinary people who Amber celebrate are working against inexorable forces which are going to marginalise them. The conflict at the heart of these two films was played out in the changing geography of Newcastle but both films are about a way of being disappearing. Old Newcastle meeting the inexorable outside forces which were going to sweep away the indigenous vitality which had made it so unique and strong.

Lee Hall

Of course there is always irony. Smith's demolition of the Byker community gave Amber's Sirkka-Liisa Konttinen her greatest photograph 'The Girl on a Spacehopper,' as part of her portrait of Byker folk in transit from slums to the Byker Wall.

A lot of their team came and settled here including Sirkka-Liisa Konttinen, who was from Finland. She loved the people here, she couldn't get past the culture. What's lovely is that Sirkka's eye is an eye of the outsider. So she sees beauty that somebody from the inside might not.

Charlie Hardwick

Amber films do great work, they have kept film-making alive for years. We still need a lot more support for arts in the region.

Ken Loach

Get Carter (1971)

Michael Caine as Jack Carter
Ian Hendry as Eric Paice
Britt Ekland as Anna
John Osborne as Cyril Kinnear
Tony Beckley as Peter the Dutchman
George Sewell as Con McCarty
Directed by Mike Hodges
Written by Ted Lewis
Music by Roy Budd

In movie terms *Get Carter* is a perfect storm. A planetary alignment of story, director, crew, cast, location and producer combined to make it number sixteen in the British Film Institute's one-hundred Greatest British Films ever made.

1971 was a watershed year in big screen crime. In the USA we were confronted by amoral cops, Harry Callaghan in *Dirty Harry* and Popeye Doyle in *The French Connection*. This realism also spread into the gangster genre. *Get Carter* captures grim reality and disillusionment with the fag-end of the 60s. Altamont had put an end to Woodstock, the Beatles had split and in London the party known as the swinging 60s was over. Organised crime in London and the regions, mythologised by the Kray twins (who had themselves flirted with the entertainment industry) tried to emulate their American mafia cousins but failed. Despite this, the arrest and conviction of the Kray twins revealed a frightening world of extortion, torture and execution.

This pattern manifested itself close to home in the North East with the apparent gangland execution of a slot machine operator near Easington. Those convicted of the crime, which related to the extortionate slot machine monopoly of working men's clubs, have always protested their innocence. The 'Slot Machine murders' are said to have partly inspired a novel, *Jack's Return Home*, by Ted Lewis. Lewis was a hard drinking, jazz piano playing, talented graphic designer from Humberside. The novel is narrated in the first person by hit man, London-based Jack Carter, as he investigates and seeks revenge for his brother Frank's untimely death. Lewis locates the action in a fictionalised Northern setting, alluding to Doncaster, Scunthorpe and other steel towns.

Jack's Return Home would be retitled *Get Carter* and the film

'Carter was the best part for me since Alfie. He was both a private eye and a ruthless gangster. Gangsters in UK films were funny or stupid - Carter was NEITHER funny or stupid. I'm nothing like Jack Carter - but i'm not a monk either.'
Michael Caine, 1971.

rights were acquired by film producer Michael Klinger whose colourful background included running Soho strip clubs and financing Polanski movies. The Carter novel suited Klinger's need for a hard hitting vérité gangster film, which would hopefully bring profits in for an ailing MGM in Europe.

Klinger's choice of director was Mike Hodges, a director grounded in current affairs and television documentary and two cutting-edge TV dramas - *Suspect* and *The Rumour*, which dealt with the impact of child abduction and journalistic truth respectively.

For a fee of £7,000 Hodges accepted the job and set about re-writing Lewis's novel for the screen. The most fundamental change was to dispense with the first person flashback narrative and to eliminate many of the back-stories, for example the feud between Carter and Eric Paice. What emerged was a fast, slick plot as Jack Carter uncovers a web of civic corruption, vice, pornography and deceit in the wake of his brother's death.

Implicit in Hodges' screenplay are references to organised crime in the North East. He had in fact thoroughly researched the 'slot machine' murders for himself when he knew he had the film commission. The gaming background is referred to in the opening scene when Carter reads a newspaper headline proclaiming GAMING WARS and also blatantly in the name of the seedy guest house 'Las Vegas', where Carter avails himself of bed and breakfast. From here he makes the first ever 'telephone' sex on film – a call to Britt Ekland. She is in fact Carter's boss's wife - their transgression will seal Jack's fate...

Newcastle in the 1970s is as much a star of the film as the cast. Klinger and Hodges drove a Cadillac and a Fiat respectively, while considering other coastal ports for locations. Hull and even Nottingham were considered but were not chosen. Mike Hodges served on a mine sweeper during his days of naval service and remembered the grittiness of the stop at North Shields. En route via Newcastle to a reconnaissance of North Shields in 1970, he saw from a taxi the changing face of the city. There was the demolition of Victorian housing, the rise of concrete apartment blocks, all part of the controversy surrounding T. Dan Smith's vision of a 'City In The Sky'. He had found Jack Carter's home:

When I got the job to direct Get Carter *I decided to research for background to flesh out and toughen Ted Lewis's story. I researched the Angus Sibbett 'slot machine murders' in this region and couldn't believe here in Newcastle there was a casino named after a Fellini film - La Dolce Vita! I wanted the city and his birth place to be so hard and uncompromising that it would only be an exception that would make him return.*

Newcastle was that place, I had found Jack's city, Carter was home.

Mike Hodges (Chris Phipps Interview, 2011 Tyne Idols Anniversary Tour)

His choice of cameraman for *Get Carter* was inspired. Wolfgang Suschitsky was a German émigré who had shot social and industrial documentaries in the late 1940s, and an Anthony Newley B movie *The Small World of Sammy Lee,* which was an unflinching portrayal of Soho club dive life. Suschitsky was a perfect choice for Hodges' panoramic views of Newcastle's high rise developments, seedy clubs and dark Tyneside alleyways and staircases. Both director and cameraman had a strong social conscience in and out of cinema and this helps to give *Get Carter* a social realism and an authenticity - every time Carter walks into a pub or a club you can sense the hostility, the curiosity and the smoke. It is this authenticity which gives *Get Carter* a freshness and a timelessness when viewed today.

The cast is perfect. Michael Caine was on his trajectory to stardom. His portrayal of the fastidious, ruthless, psychopathic hitman was the antithesis of *Alfie, The Italian Job* and *The Ipcress File's* Harry Palmer, yet his portrayal still earns our sympathy, perhaps in a way that a Western or a Jacobean tragedy might, as he sets about destroying everything for loyalty and his family name. It was his chance to nail the 70s' mobster with chilling accuracy - as Richard Attenborough had portrayed the spiv Pinky for a previous generation in Graham Greene's *Brighton Rock.*

His methods and intricate modes of revenge make him a cross between *The Terminator* and *The Count of Monte Cristo.*

The supporting cast complement Caine's performance in every way. Ian Hendry as the reptilian Eric Paice was originally cast as Carter. On producer Klinger's insistence Caine was chosen as he was a major box office draw for the US market. At the time Hendry's drink addiction didn't help matters and life imitated art when animosity developed between the two actors during script readings at the Station Hotel.

Villain Cyril Kinnear was played by playwright John Osborne, who had (ironically) created the angry young man Jimmy Porter and initiated 'New Wave' theatre and cinema of which *Get Carter* was a commercial spin-off. Osborne's performance is urbane and totally understated. We always see him hosting a wild party in his stately home - the irony is that the location used was a vacant Dryderdale Hall in Hamsterley, which had actually belonged to a gambling and slot machine Tsar, again art imitated life. Other cast members included future TV veterans George Sewell (*Special Branch*) and Brian Mosley (*Coronation Street*) as the corrupt entrepreneur Cliff Brumby. Brumby's fatal descent from the Gateshead Trinity car park is seen by many to be Get Carter's signature scene. It is said that Mosley sought priestly permission to play the part as he was a devoutly religious man.

As with *Payroll* (1961), *Get Carter* is an exercise in screen economy in style, script and plot, this economy also extends to Roy Budd's music score, written for a few hundred pounds within the £750,000 total. Roy Budd was a cool jazz piano player and a composing/arranging prodigy. The theme is performed by a trio led by him. He was recommended to Hodges by producer Klinger. Two factors are key, one is the unusual use of Indian tabla as percussion, played by Chris Karan, and the other is the eerie harpsichord/electronic theme which makes it a long-lost relative of the zither figure of the Harry Lime theme from Carol Reed's *The Third Man*. Roy Budd wisely chose not to go the conventional smoky blues/jazz route which would have been the easy way out. Instead we get this haunting, almost industrial, off-centre feel that seems to capture the concrete, the corruption, and the club and casinos that Carter is cutting his way through. Mike Hodges insisted that Budd isolated and brought out the striking electric chime theme that bookends the film's starkness. Other music includes the popular Jack Hawkins Band, who are seen playing for the dancers and smoochers at the

Caine on Westgate Road.

Oxford Galleries. The track *30 60 90*, from an album originally titled *Psychedelic Sally*, is now a sought after vinyl track. Look closely and you'll see an uncredited Jimmy Nail outside the Oxford Galleries. Another big screen debut in *Get Carter* is the great character actor Alun Armstrong who, as Keith the bar tender at The Vic and Comet, shouts the immortal question 'Is there a Mr Carter here?'

I told me Dad who was a miner, that I'd got a part in a film with Michael Caine, he said 'Get on Son, you'll be on the telly yet'
Alun Armstong, Interview with Chris Phipps, 2011 - Tyne Idols Get Carter Anniversary Tour.

Another young actor waiting in the wings was Robson Green:

There have been moments in my life which took me in a certain direction and watching Alun Armstrong in Get Carter, *when I was about nine, was one of them. There was Alun with this Geordie accent I could identify with, but he wasn't playing a token Geordie, he was a three dimensional character accessible to everyone. I sat perched on the edge of my seat taking it all in. In the back of my mind was one clear thought - maybe I can do this.*
From *Just the Beginning*, Robson Green

The *Get Carter* production designer had previously worked for Antonioni so studio bound sets weren't to be the order of the day. The famous landlady's rocking chair actually belonged to a neighbour of the 'Las Vegas' guesthouse in Coburg Street, Gateshead, where neighbours still recall filming, chatting to Caine *and* revealing he wore a body stocking for the nude and shotgun shot.

The film as ever is liberal with local geography - a pursuit behind Coburg Street suddenly ends in Newcastle's Oxford Galleries dance emporium. Pubs included the 'Vic and Comet' and the legendary 'Lang Bar' near Central station - extras were apparently plied with free drink on set. The brawl between a pub entertainer and a jealous wife was a real life confrontation exploited by Hodges. Pink Lane features too, and Margaret is shadowed from Manors Station steps to what is now Sallyport Crescent, partly preserved as the site of the City's first council accommodation. The visual power of the High Level Bridge, Long Stairs and Swing Bridge uses the legacy of *On the Night of the Fire* and *Payroll* to frame Carter perfectly as he gives chase and is chased himself. Wallsend Ferry crossing is long gone, as is the windblown St Cuthbert's Village flats development, where Jack unwittingly learns of his niece's fate - the only time we see his emotion revealed. His brutal despatch of Albert Swift in a Bookie's backyard was filmed in Hebburn - witnessed by a school friend of the future writer of *Our Friends in the North* Peter Flannery - no one believed the poor lad who stumbled on the shoot in 1970. The grim finale between Paice and Carter takes place against the primeval backdrop of Blackhall Beach, which Hodges described as a vision of hell. That location is gone and reclaimed, as is the majestic sweep on Frank Street in Benwell where Carter's brothers funeral took place - local residents objected to the authenticity of the filming, as the cortege was

At a party for the Get Carter team at the Royal Station Hotel, 25th July 1970. Mike Hodges, Michael Caine and Michael Klinger.

47

incorrectly shown leaving from the rear of the premises. You can still visit the cemetery used in the film. Frank's corpse was played by the producer's chauffeur Mr Niven who allegedly had a talent for lying *very* still.

Of course the pre-destined fatal route of Carter's fortunes once he reaches Newcastle admits him to the Film Noir hall of fame. When he confronts Cliff Brumby and warns him that 'He is a big man but out of shape' it is possibly a homage to similar lines from the Robert Mitchum classic noir *Out of the Past/Build My Gallows High*. Also it is no coincidence that Jack is reading Raymond Chandler's Noir classic *Farewell My Lovely* on his Newcastle journey. Hodges plants loads of in-jokes along the way, chiefly the Zulu shields on Kinnear's wall - a reference to Caine's past film track record.

The press and critical reception on release in 1971 ranged from mixed to muted. In Newcastle some reaction was antagonistic - understandably it wasn't an ideal tourist promotion. Some of this negative attitude survives today - the author sensed it in 2011 when the film celebrated its 40th anniversary with a location tour and Mike Hodges receiving the RTS Award before an audience at Sage Gateshead.

On release the film didn't make much money and MGM buried it in drive-ins in the USA, having re-dubbed parts in a version of 'LA Cockney'. There was even a Blaxploitation cash-in copy *Hitman*.

Get Carter was a cultural slow burning fuse, its re-release in 1999 propelled it into the upper reaches of the Brit Gangster echelons, making working class black mac menace Michael Caine, and the film itself, the definition of ultra cool, towering above even *The Long Good Friday*. Journalists from the *Independent* to lad's mags *Loaded* and *Hotdog* lauded Carter's bleak exploits - all contributing to an enshrinement of *Get Carter* as one of the UK's greatest films. A US remake with Sylvester Stallone was met with derision, even with a cameo from Michael Caine.

Mike Hodges' taxi trip in 1970 had been worth it - rightly or wrongly the film overshadows his canon of work including *Sleuth*, *Flash Gordon* and *Croupier*. For many it also remains Michael Caine's definitive performance.

Michael Caine said to me 'You're from Tyneside way? When I did Get Carter - Cockneys were always supposed to be from working class roots - after I filmed up in Newcastle I came back feeling middle class!

Ian La Frenais

I think it is interesting that Get Carter *is made by people from outside the area. We used to laugh at the continuity in the film where someone is walking down the street in Newcastle then turn a corner and are miles away. But that is not really the point.* Get Carter *could have been made anywhere in terms of its story - indeed the novel was not set in Newcastle - but what made it distinctive were the locations. Again it sits right on this cultural and historical fault line between the modernist Sixties architecture and the old Victorian conurbation which was clearly being torn apart. The film was animated by all these things being played out in the landscape - which is frankly much more interesting than anything that happens in the actual drama itself.*

Lee Hall

Jack Carter is a hard man to keep down. Northern Stage toured a new stage adaptation of Ted Lewis' novel in 2016, directed by Lorne Campbell and written by Torben Betts. Victoria Elliott, whose acting talents include *Hebburn* and *55 Degrees North* initially had reservations about portraying Margaret:

Torben used the characters in the book as starting-off points. He developed them in a modern way but they very much existed within their time and within the politics of the late 1960s. The only power that they really had in their circumstances is the power of their own sexuality and that they have to use that to the best they can in the world that they live in.

I think it is written in a much more believable, detailed human way in Torben's play than in the film and even in the book. Certainly everyone in the film just seems to take off their clothes and have sex with Michael Caine, that's their function. So it was great, we were able to take some creative licence in the play. The women are much more involved in the story and more involved in the world, much more powerful, much more intelligent and none of the women in the play have sex with Jack Carter.

Victoria Elliot

Dan's Castle (1971)

Directed by John Read
Narrated by John Donat

What went wrong with your city? the Brazilia of the North
Isn't it a pity, that no one knew it's worth
But the Civic Centre shines like money in your hand
Let's raise another glass to Dan the Plan
                    from *Dan the Plan*, written by Alan Hull, Lindisfarne

Alan Hull made a decent acting job in the BBC regional drama
Squire, written by poet/playwright Tom Pickard. *Dan the Plan* was
Hull's homage to T. Dan Smith, hailed positively as 'Mr Newcastle'
and scornfully as the 'Mouth of the Tyne.' Smith's decorating
business earned him the nickname 'One-Coat Dan' from many of
his customers. T. Dan Smith, a miner's son, is seen both as a
visionary and as a victim of corruption. As head of Newcastle City
Council he set up one of the first freestanding, and one of the most
powerful, local planning departments, crusading to sweep away the
slums of Newcastle and create in its place a 'Brasilia of the North',
a capital of arts, science and leisure beyond Westminster's reach.
Dan's Newcastle would become the capital of the North East
through a programme of aggressive regional self-development.

Rather like H.G. Wells' film of *Things To Come* (1936), Dan's
vision was of highways and high-rise flats in the sky, swirling
around the Swan House hub. In the 1960s, this was more feasible
than ever, through the revolution in building and concrete
construction. Tower block dwellings, which minimised land, were
now pre-ordered, prefabricated concrete sections brought in from

T. Dan Smith points to the future (or at least Eldon Square) near Grey's Monument.

an outside manufacturer and assembled on site. The competition to supply local authorities was cut-throat and open to financial incentives. In Newcastle, the high rise Utopia was epitomised by blocks that rose up in the Scotswood Road area - Cruddas Park flats. As other chapters in this book show, these dwellings run through Newcastle's film and television plots like Blackpool through the centre of a stick of rock. They can be seen in *A Turn Up for Tony*, *The Likely Lads*, *Wire in the Blood*, *Unconditional* and more recently *Vera*.

In the 1971 film *Dan's Castle*, Cruddas Park flats loom up in dramatic contrast to neighbouring demolition sites. As the political landscape changes so does their role in drama. By the time Terry Collier has been rehoused in the 1976 *The Likely Lads* film, his Wallsend block is a picture of urban decay. In 1996, *Our Friends in the North*'s Tosker and Mary find that their high-rise heaven is riddled with damp, so life imitates art. As Austin Donohue, the T. Dan Smith inspired character, says to his accusers, '*I didn't mix the concrete*'.

T. Dan Smith also campaigned fiercely for the regeneration of the area and finance for the arts on a local level. If you walk down to the Quayside, Dan's concrete walkways go nowhere, they end abruptly and this symbolises the outcome of a flawed vision. He had formed a public relations company and had allegedly received a million pounds in bribes to ensure that the pre-packaged construction schemes of the architect and builder John Poulson were secured for Tyneside contracts. The scandal, involving Smith, Poulson and an implied involvement by the politician Reginald Maudling was a major headline grabber in the 1970s. Smith was eventually tried for corruption and imprisoned for six years. He was always ambiguous about his guilt and ironically spent his last days on the fourteenth floor of the high-rise Mill House, Spital Tongues. He became involved, as we shall see, in a drama-documentary bearing his name and remained eloquent and confrontational to the last.

The 1971, BBC documentary *Dan's Castle* was directed by John Read and narrated by John Donat. Visually, it pulls no punches - slum dwellings, muddy allotments and ragged children are shown unflinchingly in a style redolent of Amber Films and Paul Rotha. It is a profile outlining Smith's grand visions for Newcastle and the North East. Many of them are admirable and some even came to fruition. Dan is seen being interviewed on a boat in Tynemouth and another that is travelling along the Tyne, a moving backdrop of the world he is trying to change. Most interestingly, there are artistic and architect's impressions of what the region would have looked like in the future. Whitley Bay is seen as a Riviera place of monorails, domes, sputnik-like structures, all to the score of Petula Clarkes *Downtown*. Alnmouth is seen as the Aldeborough of the future, Durham was to be linked by monorail to a new twin city with its own opera house and stadium. Also there is an event described as 'the miracle of Billingham'. The circular library of Jesmond is described as 'a diamond in the area's ear.' With total political incorrectness, another seaside resort is described as 'Buchenwald-on-Sea', where drab amusement buildings and wire fencing were to be transformed into Dan's idea of a Northern Cannes, brimming with models and yachts!

On land we see Dan driving his Mark 10 Jaguar, which was his controversial trademark transport. There are superb examples of his highly persuasive rhetoric. The documentary describes him as a 'modern crusader looking at his world'. He recalls his father's unemployment in Jarrow, when men stood and waited for work and the narrator calls for the ghosts of the Jarrow Marchers to be exorcised. Dan claims to have received four shillings and ten pence for a forty-four hour week and to have been a rebel since the age of twelve, fired by a sense of injustice at his father's unemployment.

He describes the Tyneside bridges as the strength of regional engineering, forcing the rail bridges across the river. Dan's ambitions are to make the area of international importance in a coming age of leisure, leading in the world of newspapers and television, building new bridges of culture and enterprise for the future generation. Grey Street, he claims, is perceived as 'A work of scale, proportion and grandeur felt by the ordinary man. Now we are in the century of leisure, science, technology, art, sport - happy people living and working in a good environment.' He describes, in his own words, 'A Milan of the North' costing £90 million.

'The massive task will be reversing migration from the region.' He patronisingly says that the working man talks about landscape and can tell the difference between a mountain and a block of flats. Journalistically the film acts as devil's advocate - will the population be suspicious of these proposals? Are they realistic where the staple industries have their backs against the wall and threaten a new Depression? Is all this 'A One Dan Plan?'

Prophetically *Dan's Castle* ends with a narrative comment, 'It would be a tragedy if Dan's Castle is only in the air.'

Did the film makers know something?

When the Boat Comes In (1976-1981)

Created by James Mitchell.
Writers include - James Mitchell, Sid Chaplin, Tom Hadaway and Alex Glasgow.

The television emancipation of the North East is the result of two series - *The Likely Lads* and *When the Boat Comes In*.

Significantly both starred Sunderland born James Bolam. In *The Likely Lads* he's Terry Collier, a disillusioned working class reactionary, *In When the Boat Comes In* he plays Jack Ford, a ruthless working class hero. For five years the nation took to its heart this charismatic character as a drama unfurled involving class war, politics, passion, philandering, intrigue and epic major social historical events.

In the beginning, Jack returns home from The Great War to face

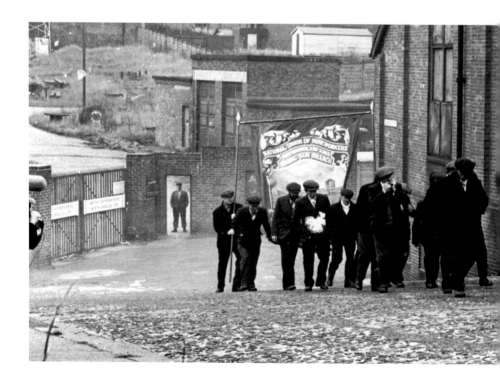

the problems of a depression hit locality known as 'Gallowshields'. By the time he dies for his political beliefs in the Spanish Civil War he has done everything from being imprisoned for his beliefs, fighting for miners' injury compensation and living in what we would call today a 'menage-a-trois.' He even gets to bootleg liquor in Prohibition-time USA and keep his cap on. The series was created by James Mitchell whose self-educated father had been mayor of South Shields. Beside creating Jack Ford, James Mitchell created the TV sleuth *Callan*.

Of *When the Boat Comes In* Mitchell said, 'Somebody who would never pick up a book of social history will watch without realising he is watching social history. Of course he isn't, he's watching a play.'

The series was a successful foil to ITV's *Upstairs, Downstairs*. Even today with the success of *Downton Abbey* British TV audiences are obsessed with dramas of social inequality. Gallowshields, a fictitious town, involved locations in Wallsend, North Shields, Whitley Bay and Howdon Road. One reviewer was

NCJ MEDIA

moved to write that it looked so genuine in its portrayals of interwar housing that you could almost contract tuberculosis from watching it.

James Bolam was joined by a who's who of Geordie acting talent including John Woodvine, Kevin Whately, Bobby Pattinson and many others. Then of course there was the unforgettable theme song sung and arranged by Alex Glasgow.

An epic that would pave the way for *Our Friends in the North* four decades on.

When the Boat Comes In *did a brilliant job of bringing politics into domestic drama. It used believable local characters and told a good story without shying away from regional issues. This was a popular drama taking in domestic and international politics. You got comedy,romance and fisticuffs!*

Writer, Brian B. Thompson

The Paper Lads
(1977-79)

Created by J.G. Holland
Writers included Ian Cullen and Sid
Chaplin.

This series followed the exploits of
Tyneside paper boys or should we say
'paper people? The gang comprised of JG,
Ian, Gog, Baz and 'Tomboy' Sam played
by Judith Pyle. Over the fourteen episodes
they witness criminal 'goings on,' solve
mysteries on allotments and one of them
is scouted by Newcastle United, which
causes internal conflict involving parental
support.

To its credit the female part of Sam is given an equal share of the plot
lines and not used in a tokenistic way. Visually *The Paper Lads* makes
very good use of what seems to be a very foggy Gateshead, possibly in
and around Bensham. The episode *Eye Witness* brilliantly employs a
shipyard location as the gang play hide and seek across a moored tanker
in pursuit of two shop burglars. Throughout the episode a knife is
glimpsed in the hands of a shipyard worker yet this potentially
threatening scene turns out to be one of him whittling a model boat. *Billy
Elliot* creator Lee Hall confesses to have been a regular viewer:

*When I grew up there were many more dramas made about the area than
there are now. It's very sad that Tyne Tees disappeared and there is no
longer a proper infrastructure of drama production here. When I was at
school there was a TV series called* The Paper Lads. *Someone from my
school, Andrew Edwards was in it so that felt very familiar. But there
wasn't one movie or series that I could completely identify with. I
suppose that's why I wrote* Billy Elliot *to try and describe what growing
up in the North East in the 80s was like. Well, a little particular sliver.*

Lee Hall

The paper shop where the gang are based is run by none other than actor
Glynn Edwards, last seen as the ill-fated Albert Swift in *Get Carter*. A
regular cast member was Newcastle's first pop star David Macbeth! *The
Paper Lads* is a fine traditional children's drama, not unrelated to the
world of boys comics and gang adventures - *Roy of the Rovers* seems to
be lurking only just around the corner.

58

The Tube (1982-87)

Tyne Tees Television for
Channel 4
Fridays 5.30-7pm
One-hundred and fifty episodes

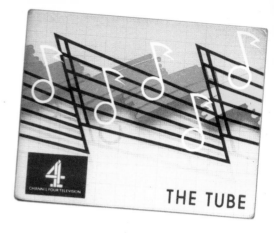

Music television has always reflected the times and trends. *Ready, Steady, Go* captured the 60s beat boom as The Who and The Kinks performed on moving platforms ploughing through a sea of dancers. *The Old Grey Whistle Test* with its 70s' cerebral presenters was the epitome of Prog Rock, as Focus, Rush and King Crimson noodled away in what looked like a broom cupboard at the BBC (*OGWT* actually did showcase new musical genres - World, Punk and the commercial version of Punk, New Wave, but most people seem to have forgotten this.)

Come the 80s, New Romantics rebooted Glam Rock, Michael Jackson saved the record business with *Thriller* and with the launch of MTV, the promotional video and the compact disc became de rigeur.

Out of Newcastle, at the dawn of Channel 4 came *The Tube*. Landing on our screens on November 5th 1982, following *Countdown*. *The Tube* took its name from the tunnel-like entrance to the Studio 5 block on City Road, opposite the Baltic Flour Mills.

Tyne Tees Television began in a furniture warehouse a little further down the road. Here, the youthful Animals, Newcastle's hopeful rivals to Merseybeat, were seen miming rather badly in front of hysterical fans and secretarial staff.

Tyne Tees had a fierce reputation for music and entertainment television. In the 70s there was *Razzamatazz* for children and *Alright Now* for rock fans. *Alright Now* had a strange, non-sequitur feeling as guest presenter Billy Connolly announced hard-core punks The Angelic Upstarts. To the dismay of London production companies and the record companies of the metropolis, Jeremy Isaacs, the incumbent head of Channel 4, awarded the

Paula Yates and Jools Holland in the tube.

music/entertainment commission to Tyne Tees Television's proposal for a show originally called *Jamming* and then re-christened *The Tube*.

For five years audiences queued and fought to get up that tubular entrance to see what unpredictable events would threaten the proceedings live on air. As its main presenters, Jools Holland and Paula Yates were key to *The Tube's* reputation. Jools was informed and credible, Paula was informed and gossipy - their style was choreographed chaos. Unlike other shows they were not disc jockeys forced to present as part of their contract or ex-pop stars attempting a new career. Jools and Paula were insiders hosting a club gig exclusive to the cavernous Studio 5. *The Tube* ran twenty-six weeks of the year and it was 'appointment-to-view' television. Other notable presenters were actress Lesley Ash and journalist Muriel Gray – but it was Jools' and Paula's show.

Programme one opened with a heavily pregnant Paula, a sparkler-brandishing Jools Holland and Sunderland's Toy Dolls tearing into a wine bar homage entitled *She Goes to Fino's*. The first show ended with The Jam's last ever TV performance and thus *The Tube* set out its stall.

Musically, *The Tube* became a talent hoovering machine, rebooting the career of Tina Turner, providing an early showcase for Madonna, discovering Fine Young Cannibals, Frankie Goes To Hollywood, Paul Young, Twisted Sister, The Proclaimers, as well as providing a platform for reggae, African and (patronisingly titled) world music. Newcastle provided unwitting locations to video shoots for The Smiths in an upstairs pub/restaurant and Bananarama in the Gosforth Park Hotel cocktail bar for *Robert de Niro's Waiting*. The breadth of music was staggering from Iggy Pop to Grace Jones to Elton John - <u>all live</u>.

The programme's booking policy was extremely democratic and unsigned acts got the same artistic and budgetary treatment as the bill-toppers. A typical line-up is exemplified in 1983, series two, programme one - Tina Turner, Heaven 17, Eurythmics, PIL and Billy Bragg. The Egypt Cottage pub, which adjoined the studio, was often co-opted into the programme running order and became known as 'Studio Six'. It was not unknown for a casual drinker to be confronted by the sight of Ozzy Osborne being interviewed in a

Top: *Back stage with Billy Bragg and Bono.* Middle: *Chris Phipps with Little Richard.*
Right: *Paula Yates and Dave Stewart.*

coffin in the bar. Comedy in the 80s was a new form of rock and roll and it was very much a part of *The Tube's* formula, as Rick Mayall vomited at the camera on City Road, French and Saunders posed as Paul Young fans and an unknown Vic Reeves flew on a 'Kirby' wire in the last programme's parody of *Celebrity Squares*.

When *The Tube* was good it was very, very good. When *The Tube* was bad it was awful. Its irreverence, shambolic quality and occasional profanity nearly pulled it off the air at least twice in five years. Pre-recording would have diminished a show fiercely proud of its live ethos. The last show ended with Duran Duran in 1987. They were brought in as a last minute replacement for an ailing James Brown. U2 paid homage with a Hank Williams valediction.

The Tube turned Newcastle into the capital of cool for at least five years, but its potential was never followed through. *The Roxy*, an attempt to rival *Top of the Pops* was a valiant failure. *The Tube's* legacy can be seen in *The Word, TFI Friday* and the chat show style of Jonathan Ross, Russell Brand and the usual suspects.

Studio Director Gavin Taylor went on to direct some of the iconic live in-concert performances from Queen to Michael Jackson. His *Tube* film of U2 at RedRocks is seen as their definitive performance on film.

Film director Geoff Wonfor went on to direct the Beatle's *Anthology* and further Jools Holland projects.

Paula Yates died in tragic circumstances and Jools Holland hosts his eclectic *Later with...* for the BBC.

In a city not known for entrepreneurial talent *The Tube* was a maverick independent programme. It did what it did without apology and this spirit will emerge later in the book. In the year *The Tube* launched, the Live Theatre found its home on the Quayside and it signalled a cultural regeneration along the river that inspired Eric Burdon, Alan Hull, Sting and Mark Knopfler.

The Tube's Studio 5 was mothballed and eventually demolished along with the rest of the City Road site. The Tube waxwork family, who occupied the opening titles, and the original neon sign now belong to Newcastle's Discovery Museum where a permanent *The Tube* exhibit is planned.

Top: *Moving out.* Right: *Tyne Tees Television on City Road, the Egypt Cottage or 'Studio Six' on the right.*

NCJ MEDIA

Auf Wiedersehen Pet (1983-2004)

Timothy Spall as Barry Taylor
Jimmy Nail as Oz Osborne
Tim Healy as Dennis Patterson
Kevin Whately as Neville Hope
Christopher Fairbank as Albert Moxey
Pat Roach as Bomber Busbridge
Gary Holton as Wayne Norris
Julia Tobin as Brenda Hope
Created by Frank Roddam

Series writing credits:
Ian La Frenais (33 episodes, 1983-2004)
Dick Clement (26 episodes, 1983-2004)
Franc Roddam (21 episodes, 1983-2004)
Stan Hey (6 episodes, 1983-1986)
Bernie Cooper (1 episode, 1984)
Francis Megahy (1 episode, 1984)

If *The Likely Lads* captured the zeitgeist of the 60s and 70s, *Auf Wiedersehen Pet* mirrored the Thatcherite 80s from the building site. This series was the brainchild of Franc Roddam, a Teessider who has made iconic contributions to film and television. They range from the screen version of The Who's *Quadrophenia* which he directed, the first 'fly-on-the-wall' documentary series *The Family* and eventually to the demystification of cookery in *Masterchef*.

Roddam was fascinated (via the direct experiences of an old friend) by tales of North East men who, faced with unemployment in the recession at home, were forced to seek jobs in Germany. Surely, he thought, this had great potential for film or television drama, the exploits of strangers in a strange land. Willy Russell was first approached, but passed, and the topic went onto the backburner. Under different circumstances he eventually presented the idea to Dick Clement and Ian La Frenais who were extremely enthusiastic despite a reasonably fruitless research trip to Germany.

In *Auf Wiedersehen Pet* they once again created their unique mixture of drama and comedy, revolving around seven characters -

they are Bomber - a gentle West Country giant, Moxey - an enigmatic Scouser, Barry - a pedantic Midlander, Wayne - a chirpy womanising cockney, and of course a trio of Geordies: Dennis - who is seen as the shop steward and the voice of reason despite the loss of his business and marriage, Neville - a hen-pecked homesick husband and Oz - an uncouth xenophobic character created as a total antithesis to his workmates.

Oz was portrayed by Jimmy Nail, who apart from an uncredited part in *Get Carter* had never acted professionally. It is ironic that Oz who once used the expression 'He's about as welcome as a fart in an astronaut's suit' was taken to the nation's heart.

NCJ MEDIA

We really did not approve of Oz. We really tried to write him as a person it was impossible to approve of. He behaved appallingly to his wife and son, never sent them any money. His attitude to Germans was terrible. He was politically incorrect before the phrase was even invented. But what happened? People started to like him and once we met Jimmy we started to like him too. Then in a way he got softened a bit. Maybe we were seduced away from our original intentions.

Dick Clement
From *That's Living Alright - The Auf Wiedersehen Pet Story*

In the lifespans of the successive series the whole gang in different ways find themselves collectively forced out of their comfort zones, initially in a prison-like labourer's hut block in Germany and then as the years go by in Spain, America and Cuba. Their exploits are well documented elsewhere and there is an *Auf Wiedersehen Pet* Society. A favourite storyline of mine is the hilarious attempt to smuggle pornographic material in coffins back to the UK.

The core of its success and its appeal is that Clement and La Frenais give the working class a dignity mainly through brilliantly written and observed conversation which we eavesdrop upon as they scheme, console, worry, bicker and survive as outsiders in other cultures. For each individual, home in Blighty can be where the heart or the hatred lies waiting. The *Auf Wiedersehen Pet* gang embody many facets of the English (and its regional variations) abroad. Much is made elsewhere in this book of Geordie characters and communities being resistant to outsiders, here on building and construction sites across Europe they find that the tables are turned. Dennis, Neville and Oz are themselves the outsiders. The case has been made that Oz is an unreconstructed North Easterner whose lineage includes Terry Collier, Jack Ford *and* Jack Carter.

Terry (Collier), Oz and Jack Carter are of a type. That both Terry and Oz are humorous figures, and Carter a disturbing one, indicates there is a general uneasiness here about the sort of masculinity they between them represent. Yet also evident is an enduring fascination with the sheer awfulness of these people, suggesting that this particular stereotype still has a good deal of life left in it.

From *When the Going Gets Tough* by Peter Hutchings

The source of Neville's homesickness is rarely seen in the series because of course they are always abroad, however, in one very poignant scene, Oz and his estranged son, Rod, walk and talk along Prince Consort Way at the Royal Quays Marina and say farewell to each other at Sandgate. Once again the Quayside perfectly frames human drama. There are also glimpses of Akenside, Dean Street, the Bigg Market and Dog Leap Stairs, but from economic necessity London was often used to double as Newcastle.

There is an apocryphal story that a piece of the Berlin Wall bore the graffiti inscription *Demolished by Oz!*

Mention should be made of Michael Chaplin's very popular *Grafters* portraying brother builders living and loving in London - again another dramatic context for the skill drain.

A course in brick laying for Christopher Fairbank, Kevin Whately and Pat Roach.

Jossy's Giants (1986-87)

If Newcastle United scouted from the ranks of *The Paper Lads* then they missed a whole potential side known as *Jossy's Giants*. This series followed the varied fortunes of the Glipton Grasshoppers filmed in a fictional Pennine area, in reality Oldham and Stalybridge. They are coached by Joswell 'Jossy' Blair a former child football star who was invalided out of Newcastle Football Club as an adult.

In a classic episode the Grasshoppers get to meet their heroes when they get to visit St James's Park. They are treated to extraordinarily wooden performances by Bobby Charlton and Bryan Robson - clearly a warning to the producers of the future epic *Goal!* The whole concept was created by darts commentator and Yorkshire renaissance man Sid Waddell.

Geordie Racer (1988)

This short lived series starring Kevin Whately and Madeleine Newton was a Newcastle based story of pigeon fanciers and runners set against the background of the Great North Run. Its hero was 'Spuggy' Hilton, owner of the champion 'Blue Flash' who along with Janie discover that pigeons are being used for criminal intelligence. Made under the auspices of BBC's *Look and Read* educational programmes, *Geordie Racer* proved to be an unusual gritty entry into the genre and was much loved by teachers and pupils. It is ironic that the following year Newcastle would be the setting for a revolution in youth programming - *Byker Grove*.

Stormy Monday (1988)

Melanie Griffith as Kate
Tommy Lee Jones as Cosmo
Sting as Finney
Sean Bean as Brendan
James Cosmo as Tony
Directed by Mike Figgis

Stormy Monday is a tale of territorial, invasive corporate crime.
One of the key notes of this movie literally IS jazz. Ever since
Bernstein's score for *The Man with the Golden Arm*, jazz, as a
music form, came to imply subversion and criminality, and this film
is no exception - pulsing through the city, the plot, the director and
at least one of its cast.

The film's director and writer Mike Figgis was born in
Newcastle and his passion for cinema was fuelled by clandestine
visits to the Tyneside Cinema. His route to materialising *Stormy
Monday* was a long, hard road strewn with chance, defeat and
dogged determination. Figgis was a jazz player and had been a
member of local band The Gas Board whose line-up boasted a then
undiscovered Brian Ferry. For a decade, Figgis lived as a multimedia performer as part of The People Show, a London-based
performance group. Rejected by the National Film School, the
persistent Figgis created a performance art piece *Redheugh*, which
was semi-autobiographical, and eventually directed an
extraordinary avant garde short film *The House* starring Stephen
Rea and Nigel Hawthorne, set in Mid-Europe.

Mindless Violence, his script depicting a Tyneside gangland
execution would eventually mutate into the plot for a movie
originally titled *Around Midnight*. Discovering that there was
already a film with this title (a jazz bio-pic), the new title emerged
as *Stormy Monday*, inspired by the legendary T. Bone Walker blues
classic. *Stormy Monday* would secure finance from Channel 4 and
British Screen. The story of his securing American finance for the
balance of the budget is a saga worthy of a movie itself.

The film owes everything to its central creative trio of talent.
director, composer and writer Mike Figgis, producer Nigel
Stafford-Clark and cameraman Roger Deakins. The trio had
proved their worth already in *The House*.

The Newcastle depicted in *Stormy Monday* is a gentrified,
designer-led city. The Quayside and much of the city centre was

finding itself bathed in neon light as a new partying city culture emerged. Wine bars appeared like the head of the Hydra and flashy think-tank reports described Newcastle centre as a culture of vertical drinking where ear-piercing sound systems encouraged alcohol intake. There was a floating nightclub on the foggy Tyne. As profits soared there were cultural casualties, chiefly live music, as musical distraction was not to be encouraged at night. Grey's Club and The Stage Door held out against the tide of cocktails and Grolsch beer. In 1988, into this arena comes the plot and the cast of *Stormy Monday*. In a way the film does for cinema what *The Tube* did for music television - it raged in glossy-shoulder padded garishness and chaos, and didn't care.

The underlying plot of *Stormy Monday* centres on outsiders attempting to annexe and invade Tyneside. This was previously a focus of *The Long Good Friday* where gangster Harold is courting American mob interests in London's docklands. Now it's the turn of the Quayside, the target for the ambitious American businessman Cosmo, a man with more than a hint of organised crime connections. Standing in his way is the gritty Geordie entrepreneur Finlay, whose venue The Quay Club is the last bastion of jazz in the city. Finlay knows that in some ways his musical era and interests are coming to an end, but nevertheless he has other clubs in his empire.

As the film heads towards a climactic showdown between Finlay and Cosmo, the background setting is a promotional American week in Newcastle. There are two sub-plots, one involving a love affair between Finlay's janitor Brendan and Cosmo's escort companion Kate, and the other involving the Kracow Jazz Ensemble who unwittingly find themselves playing the American National Anthem.

Casting is spot on, Tommy Lee Jones, with a face like Easter Island statue, is the urbane, menacing Cosmo. Finlay gives Sting an acting role to complement his mid-eighties superstardom. Operating from Akenside, which doubled as the Quay Club office, art imitated life as Sting came from a Tyneside jazz background before becoming a proto-reggae punk in the Police. Sean Bean cuts an edgy figure as Brendan, a part originally intended for Tim Roth. Melanie Griffith, fresh from her success in *Something Wild*, excelled as a troubled Kate.

As with *Get Carter*, Newcastle locations rival the cast visually for the starring role. It is Mike Figgis's tribute to film noir colliding with the visions of artist Edward Hopper. For him Newcastle, his home city, was the natural inspiration and successor to the noirish cities of Chicago and New York:

The scale of architecture and of the bridges on the Tyne was very like Chicago. When I toured with The People Show and had gone to Chicago and New York I was very struck by how much they reminded me of Newcastle, just the scale was bigger.

Here I was in Newcastle, my home town, we had taken a whole derelict area of a very beautiful section of the city and by turning it into a film set had demonstrated what a visually interesting thing it could be. In fact, if you go down to that section now you would basically see my film set...there was a local hero kind of pride thing going on for me which I have never experienced since.

Mike Figgis, from *My First Movie*

Perhaps looking to their future careers, Sting and Mike Figgis on Sandhill.

NCJ MEDIA

Much of the film is photographed on the run during limited night-time hours. The most stunning sequences include Cosmo and Finlay face to face at dawn on the High Level Bridge and the detonation of a Jaguar at Sandgate. The locations were meticulously selected by Mike Figgis and unusually formed a geographically correct route from Central Station to the Quayside, unlike other films which 'cut and shut' with geographic reality. Local residents were taken aback at the sight of French sailors fighting over call girls at the bottom of Dean Street. Amidst the neon gloss that pervades the film, the meeting of Brendan and Kate is pure Edward Hopper. Figgis's own jazz score is vastly underrated.

The movie was seen by many as a triumph of style over substance, Alexander Walker called it 'the crudest calling card to Hollywood' and so it proved as Figgis went on to helm *Leaving Las Vegas* and *Internal Affairs*, as well as beginning a digital arts career and having a digital suite at his beloved Tyneside Cinema named after him.

Oh yes the Royal Station Hotel is there again!

One of the best things in the film
was shot after one of the worst
nights of filming. The scene where
Tommy Lee Jones and Sting are
walking across the bridge at the
crack of dawn, we grabbed that on
the run after a night of filming in
the rain the final scene outside the
nightclub.
Mike Figgis Collected Screenplays

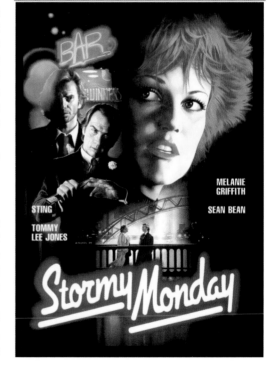

And when I look at England, in
particular this area, this once great
area, I see that the going is tough -
and I see that it's time that the
tough got going - this area requires
major surgery.
from the Stormy Monday script
from Mike Figgis Collected
Screenplays

Byker Grove (1989-2006)

Byker Grove produced by Zenith North/Zenith Entertainment for BBC

The Tube had revolutionised the way pop music was consumed on the small screen. Following the series demise, *The Tube's* co-creator Andrea Wonfor, heading up the newly formed Zenith North in Newcastle, turned her attention from pop music to shaking up children's afternoon drama. Her allies in this were *Coronation Street* writer Adele Rose and producer/director Matthew Robinson (who would eventually be known as the 'Pope of Soap') fresh from putting *Eastenders* into every front room.

Byker Grove was originally aimed at eight to eleven year olds, but after commission by the BBC it targeted twelve to sixteen year olds. From 1989 to 2006 it captivated young adults, teenagers and, if the truth be known, their parents as well. Unlike *Grange Hill* the action and the stories were not focussed on a school, but a youth centre in a fictitious part of Newcastle. Despite the title it was filmed nowhere near Byker but actually in the west end of Newcastle at Benwell. Most of the action takes place within the walls of the youth centre filmed at The Mitre, a former episcopalian residence which had also seen life as a pub and a club and the author actually saw bands there auditioning for *The Tube* in the 80s.

So successful was the series that these premises were permanently licensed out by the BBC to film and produce the series.

There are a number of reasons for the incredible success of *Byker Grove*. Story lines didn't patronise the young audience with the stock themes of footballing, burglary and allotments. The cast were local and didn't speak in Geordie accents learned in a drama school. The story lines didn't shy away from issues which included homophobia, teenage pregnancy, homelessness, drug addiction and the general unfairness of life ranging from accidental death to mental illness. The nation took many of the characters to heart and watched the ups and downs of their lives mainly in, but sometimes outside 'The Grove.'

The two most durable characters were of course PJ and Duncan who would eventually emerge as the colossi of British Light Entertainment - Ant and Dec. They grew up in front of us in a place that was focussed on youth, not the classroom - the Byker

Right: The ever-present backdrop to Byker Grove was Benwell's The Mitre.

NCJ MEDIA

NCJ MEDIA

Grovers inhabited a world that was exclusively theirs, not full of clichéd teachers and adult figures - the audience were made to feel not just observers but members of this club - Newcastle may be the location, but the teenage fortunes and problems had no boundaries.

Simon Heath was story editor from 1993-1996 and wrote several episodes in 1996 and 1997:

Byker Grove had a feel of urban realism, it never felt or appeared studio bound. Matthew Robinson (Producer) achieved very high production values on a low budget.

The series attracted huge press. In 1994 Gary and Noddy had the first gay kiss on children's television at a five o'clock viewing time! Characters tended to be written out when they were sixteen - with the exception of Ant and Dec. I felt it got harder writing as the series went into the noughties, but it always managed to capture a mood and even got mums and dads watching too. It is vital to remember that this could only have been made by an independent prodcution team. There was something anti-establishment about it - in the spirit of that other Newcastle production *The Tube*!

Brian B. Thompson was *Byker Grove's* most prolific writer, writing fifty episodes over twelve series. According to Brian:

Looking back at those early episodes, *Byker Grove* was a fascinating mix. It had a visual realism you just didn't see on TV, but the storylines were more familiar from the soap world. It was like Ken Loach had got the gig at *Home and Away*.

Working on it, you found fact and fiction crossing over all the time. The cast were playing characters close to their real selves and our job was to create stories that could have come from their own lives. There was an overlap too between the fictional *Byker Grove* youth club and its real-life setting, The Mitre (also our production HQ and a second home to everyone on the show). Both were Geordie utopias of sorts: safe, welcoming, sealed communities ruled over by benevolent dictators, whether youth leader or producer. That unique old building was like a Geordie Camelot, keeping at bay all but the most persistent BBC execs, nervously clutching their return tickets to King's Cross. Even back then, that level of independence was rare in TV. Of course, it could never last – but getting away with it for seventeen years wasn't a bad effort.

Top: *Filming in the Freeman Hospital.* Right: *In the Bigg Market, 1993.*

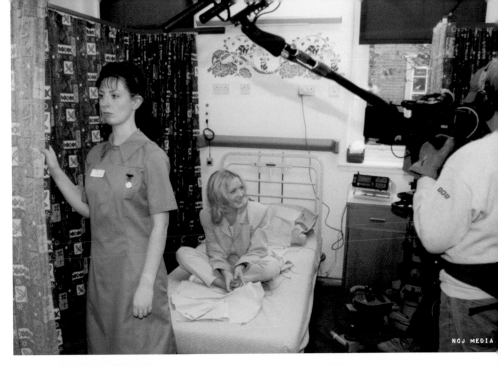

Byker Grove was famous for tackling social issues – homosexuality, contraception, sudden death, dangerous driving (by kids!). This reflected its pioneering edge and wide audience range (all the way up to late teens). But that gradually changed as greater moral and commercial pressures bore down on the world of children's TV, forcing it to separate off into a safer, ring fenced world. Our upper audience age fell to eight or nine years old, so doing stories about condoms and the like quickly disappeared off the agenda.

Yet it was never all about controversial storylines. I remember Matthew Graham, (writer who went on to create *Life on Mars*) taking me aside just after my first Byker story conference. He said that the big stories might get the headlines but when you talk to our viewers what they remember is 'when the goat farted'. This referred to a classic and often re-used story. A Grover finds an animal roaming, lost. They take it to the Grove but the youth leader says it has to go so they keep it hidden. After some scatological and frankly fart-based behaviour, it's re-discovered by the youth leader, who throws a radgie and hoofs it out. Just in time, the real owner turns up and it's sad farewells all round for the loveable, if smelly, rogue. I remember writing a version of this involving a llama. Famously, children and animals can be difficult to work with and so it proved. I get a call from the production office the day before filming. 'The llama keeps trying to bite the kids, we cannae use it'. The animal wrangler was asked what other

NCJ MEDIA

creatures are available. 'A hamster, and nowt else', comes the reply. That was a long night!

Fun was a vital part of the *Byker Grove* mix. The Geordie sense of humour - irreverent and levelling – was very strong in the show and a natural asset for many of the actors. Ant and Dec radiated that sort of sunshine and developed it into a phenomenal career, but they were far from alone. Last time I looked two Byker alumni were playing leads in long-running US TV dramas. Canny good like.

From dinosaurs and Pokémon cards to Robot Wars and heavy metal, every fad my kids got into went in the show. I also manged to fit some of my own in – how many other kids' programmes did a lengthy, multi-layered storyline about greyhound racing?

The story that sticks in my mind is the death of Ben. He was a very popular character, played by Andrew Haydn Smith, a lovely bloke and great looking guy so we didn't want to let him go, even though he had become way too old to be at The Grove. We made him a youth leader but it didn't suit his bad boy image, so we took him on a long journey in which he tried to reform his younger brother, met his absent Dad and then went off the rails. It was during this story that, perhaps jogged by his character's surname (Carter), we did our homage to *Get Carter*, complete with using the iconic car park location and immortal 'outta shape' line. Ben was finally run over and killed, but it wasn't all bad 'cos Andrew's still enjoying a great afterlife as a presenter, actor and model.

A less happy ending was when the show got cancelled. But it lives on: 'Ooo Byker, Byker, Byker Grove', still gets sung at me by the unlikeliest of people and some southerners continue to think it was about a bike gang, presumably a dyslexic one.

Brian B. Thompson (Writer)

Many actors served their acting apprenticeships as cast members on *Byker Grove* including Ant & Dec, Donna Air, Jill Halfpenny, Chelsea Halfpenny, Andrew Haden-Smith and Charlie Hunnam. Tyneside actress Charlie Hardwick, later to become Val Pollard in *Emmerdale*, also served in the ranks at 'The Grove':

I was in *Byker Grove* for four years, I did two stints in it, the first was as Dec's mother and then several years later I was reinvented as Sian the youth worker, which was just after Ant and Dec left. *Byker Grove* was great and kids still talk about it today, grown men will see me and shout 'it's Sian off *Byker Grove*!' *Byker Grove* was edgier, it wasn't set in a school but a youth club. It wasn't really about the adults it was about the kids and occasionally you had to be there to lend a bit of support, but really they got on with it behind closed doors. That was its strength. It was stories about young people and featuring young people. The cast were just ordinary kids.

Charlie Hardwick

Many would argue that The Mitre was the real star of the series as Location Manager, Christine Llewellyn-Reeve remembers:

It is difficult to pick out a specific memory about the legend that is *Byker Grove*. There are so many. I joined the production for its final three years. The first year as the Location Manager, and the last two years as the Production Manager then Line Producer. The promotion was a big step up in responsibility and quite a challenge.

I think the most important 'memory' is the Mitre itself where the programme was filmed and produced. This old Bishop's Palace was both fictionally the Byker Grove Youth Centre, as well as our Production Offices, editing and post-production base. It was so special it was really a central 'character' in itself if not a star in its own right. Quirky, difficult to manage at times, striking appearance, with a fascinating history and possibly a ghost. It was friendly, warm and exciting becoming a second 'home' for cast and crew, and the place where a lot of 'unknown' young actors literally grew up. It was huge fun to be based there although due to its age, a constant challenge to maintain its upkeep. It had been a pub before the BBC took it over, so there was no problem in converting the integral chapel into the main Youth Centre activities hall. The other huge rooms with magnificent windows became the various recreational areas of the club, and we could also build temporary sets inside the building due to its high ceilings and spacious proportions. The staircase was particularly impressive although I am not sure the Bishops would have approved of the huge jungle murals and animals that adorned the magnificent sweep of the stairs over two floors! The Mitre was operational virtually all year round, a very unusual thing in the Film and TV industry. The grounds were also a joy, except when it was raining or when I had to deal with an infestation of Japanese Knot Weed!

'The Mitre' is hidden away in Benwell in the West End of Newcastle, even some of the locals didn't know that one of their favourite shows was being created behind the fences at the bottom of their gardens. They must have wondered from time to time, about all the strange goings on, the arrival of convoys of action vehicles, police cars and a pink Cadillac, and especially when we created a full sized replica of a Roman trebuchet which catapulted flour (don't ask!) clearly visible from our neighbours windows or when we placed huge green fabric screens in the trees and had enthusiastic trained youngsters bouncing on trampolines appearing above the said fences turning somersaults in front of the chroma key screens to give the impression they were flying in a homage to *Crouching Tiger, Hidden Dragon*. *Byker Grove* was a triumph of creativity over a limited budget which resulted in finding ways of giving the best on screen values and realizing what could seem like impossible script demands through sheer invention.

Some locations used in *Byker Grove* were 'old friends' as they appeared in nearly every script. The 'homes' of the key characters, and other locations were revisited year after year, in a diversity of areas from Montague Avenue and Jesmond to Denton Burn and Coxlodge, from Cat and Dog Shelters to big supermarkets, from tiny terraces to The Gate and from major hospitals to The Sage to name just a few. Not many know that *Byker Grove* rented a terrace house in the Byker Wall Estate for many years. The views from this small but perfectly formed Council House were stunning, taking in the iconic curve of the river and all the Bridges and made it absolutely worthwhile to re-visit every year and see if we could break the world record for how many crew and cast, cameras and lights we could get into a small space.

Over the three years I was involved we must have filmed in nearly six hundred locations. I inherited a production that had been operational for fifteen years, with virtually the same team, many, like me were ex-Tyne Tees Television employees who had worked together for many years. The majority of us were North East born and bred with a huge pride in featuring the region. I and the public reaped the benefit of an almost extended family atmosphere and commitment to the region and production. We prided ourselves in being as professional and friendly as possible and made sure we protected 'our own patch'. I can honestly say we were always welcomed back for another year of a *Byker Grove* invasion by the public, the Councils and the Police.

Byker Grove kept Newcastle, Gateshead and the North East firmly and proudly in the eye of the nation for eighteen fantastic years.

One of the biggest scenes of the last series, this was a 'money shot' sequence involving all the cast in a fictional 'protest ride' on bicycles through the Newcastle city centre and ending up with forty cyclists in confrontation with the Police and Public in the narrow section of High Bridge Street between Grey Street and Pilgrim Street. As you can imagine, this took a lot of setting up. We were allowed to take over Grey Street from the Monument down to the junction with High Bridge Street as long as we did it early on a Sunday morning and with the help of the Police. Once we were in High Bridge Street we were allowed to film for the rest of the day in this controlled area and in negotiation with the restaurants and pubs.

It was an absolute privilege to stand in Grey Street, on a beautiful Sunday morning, looking up towards the Monument and the Theatre Royal framed in Cornflower blue skies, in what is considered to be one of the most beautiful street vistas in the UK and not a vehicle in sight. The shot of over forty bikes and riders coming down Grey Street went without a hitch and we moved to the more complex action in High Bridge Street. What we hadn't counted on was that the day proved to be the hottest of the summer. Health and Safety is always of paramount importance, especially when filming with children and as the day went on, it became a challenge to keep everyone cool, hydrated and alert. The tar between the cobbles of the street actually started to melt, the bike tyres got so hot they began to deflate - not helpful at all to the action! We did what we could under the circumstances and carried on through this till seven o'clock in the evening finally accepting that we could do no more and have to make the most of the material we had managed to shoot. What made the day possible was the generosity of the pubs and cafes who allowed us to give rest breaks out of the heat beyond those refuges originally planned and the pre-arranged supply of super food in the meal breaks for all. The Tyneside Cinema Tea Rooms and Fitzgeralds have retained my vote for great food and hospitality beyond the call of duty. I think some of the usual punters were a bit surprised to see large numbers of children drinking gallons of orange juice in their local in Fitzgeralds that day.

Another memorable weekend being allowed to film an 'operation' sequence at the Freeman Hospital. Working within rigid weekend available times in the surgical outpatients ward and Theatre with professionals on duty with us, guiding us through the authentic and

CHRISTINE LLEWELLYN-REEVE

CHRISTINE LLEWELLYN-REEVE

CHRISTINE LLEWELLYN-REEVE

correct way to carry out the procedures. We also filmed ambulance sequences outside the landmark exteriors. The Hospital Trust always gave us huge support when having to find these difficult locations and we were only too happy to film within their understandably strict regulations and time availabilities. Newcastle College also allowed us to film in downtimes in their amazing state of the art training wards out in Coach Lane. The length of time we filmed in the region enabled us to forge lasting connections with some of the key public services and communities in Newcastle and Gateshead and to reflect the community as well as being a part of it

Christine Llewellyn-Reeve

Inevitably tastes change and the viewing habits of the noughties caught up with the series and it was decommissioned in 2006. Sadly, Zenith entertainment went into liquidation the following year. It is alleged that Ant and Dec now own the rights to the series which made them five o'clock stars.

Spender (1991-1993)

Jimmy Nail as Freddie Spender
Sammy Johnson as Kenneth Norman 'Stick' Oakley
Berwick Kaler as Dan Boyd
Denise Welch as Frances Spender
Brendan Healy as Eric
Created by Ian La Frenais and Jimmy Nail

Spender in its pilot form was written by Ian La Frenais. The majority of episodes over this highly successful series were written by its star Jimmy Nail, following a year's mentoring by La Frenais, which involved Nail's exile to Los Angeles. As with many success stories in entertainment there is a wild card involved, in this case Nail's ambition to play a policeman in the North East was a second choice when his original proposal to dramatise the story of the Stephenson steam dynasty was rejected. It is also claimed in his autobiography that this was the first totally North East based drama production.

The first day's filming was an absolute thrill, I stood behind the camera to watch and listen as the actors delivered lines I'd written. They worked. It was odd filming on the street I'd grown up on.
Jimmy Nail, A Northern Soul.

Freddie Spender was a name coined by Nail based on an R&B/TexMex singer Freddie Fender:

I said 'Jimmy you can't call anybody Freddie' he said 'It's my son's name' and he stuck with it, remember this - Jimmy's a perfectionist - so Freddie Spender it was. We really got to show a lot of the North East - moody stuff. I had always loved the shots of Oz and his son in Sandgate by the bridges in Auf Wiedersehen Pet.
Ian La Frenais Interiew with Chris Phipps 2016

Spender works as an undercover detective in Newcastle and the North East. His bosses in London decide to relocate him back to his home patch following the death of his colleague while on a stakeout in London. His return home - a 'Carter'- like train journey in episode one - is a reluctant one. He seems also aware of corruption as one of his superiors says to him, 'You're not the first copper to think things aren't right.'

Spender is surrounded by sharply-drawn characters. Closest to him is a local musician, played by ex-80s Dance Class guitarist Tony McAnaney, his screen character embittered and trying to adjust to the onset of multiple sclerosis. In real life McAnaney composed the successful theme tune. As with all things connected to Jimmy Nail, music is not very far away in the sub-plot.

Spender's accomplice in the shadowy world he inhabits is 'Stick' Oakley, a man he describes as 'having never been East of Wallsend'. Stick is a Dickensian, slightly lovable ex-jailbird who can sound out and investigate under the stones that Spender overturns with his foot. He has a wry attitude - when he is scoffing a free meal in a hotel following a spell in prison for petty crime he describes the buffet as 'a tax rebate'. Spender and Stick (played by the late Sammy Johnson) are a classic coupling of television sleuths. For me they are on a par with *Callan* and his his sidekick 'Lonely', characters also created by a Tynesider - James Mitchell.

Denise Welch plays Spender's estranged wife and the late Brendan Healey, lugubrious as ever, portrays her future husband. On the odd occasion that Spender drops his hard-bitten guard it is when he sees his own family taking a new direction for the future. In a scene that replicates one from *Stormy Monday* his ex-wife is the victim of an explosion on the Quayside. Spender realises that he has exposed his own family to the forces he is fighting.

Another key character is his local police contact DS Dan Boyd played by Berwick Kaler. Boyd is a world-weary desk-bound copper who is Spender's only above-board contact from the twilight world where he operates. 'Spender? He's on the outside - he works on his own.'

For me, Spender is a transatlantic version of 'Dirty' Harry Callaghan. He has a strongly focused sense of street justice but has no time for niceties, rules or regulations. He gets the job done with no compromises. Spender is lank-haired, insubordinate and surly. He is surrounded by an acute sense of loneliness as he says, 'Can we leave it alone my being alone?' He assures someone else, 'I look miserable all the time.' Locations emphasise his loneliness - in situ on the Castle Keep roof, on the rain-sodden Quayside dwarfed by the Tyne Bridge, and isolated by Marsden Rock. It is epitomised when he is seen playing harmonica on a ferry and also by a classic theme based around a whistle harking back to ITV's series *Ghost Squad*. Nail's humour pervades the scripts, particularly when it is aimed at the gentrification of Newcastle in the 90s, something that Spender scorns. 'Get rid of those beanbag chairs!' he shouts. He also tells that a cafe bistro provides what he describes as 'Great scrambled tofu!

Spender's undercover roles range from oil rig worker to a roadie for Mark Knopfler. (In reality Knopfler produced Nail's mega-hit *Big River*.)

It's slightly like Miami Vice *meeting a crumbling post-industrial Newcastle.*

Brian B. Thompson

There is also a rich stream of plot lines ranging from disappearing footballers, bill-posting wars, tape bootlegging and a corrupt boys' home being run by a modern Fagin. In one remarkable scene Spender declares war on the main coke dealer by emptying coke bags in front of him.

The series is also a casting call for a repertory of North East actors or those associated with the area. You can spot Rodney Bewes, Timothy Spall, Frances Tomelty, Mike Elliot and future Grammy winner Bob Smeaton.

It is a long journey from the Jarrow Crusade to Jimmy Nail as Spender, investigating mayhem among the yuppies

Alan Plater from *Geordies*

Jimmy Nail's musical talents and ambitions would fully re-surface in his creation Jed Shepperd, the tragi-comic Geordie Country and Western singer who makes the journey from Newcastle to Nashville in the extremely popular *Crocodile Shoes* (1992-94)

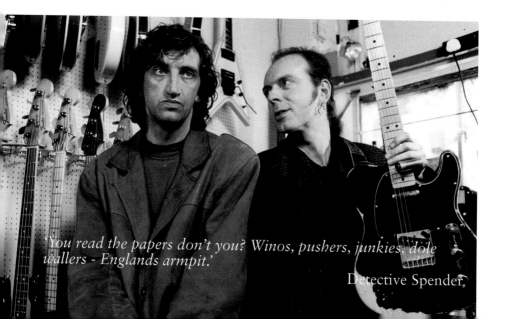

'You read the papers don't you? Winos, pushers, junkies, dole wallers - Englands armpit.'

Detective Spender

Paper Marriage (1993)

Gary Kemp as Aiden
Joanna Trepechinska as Alicja
Also featuring Rita Tushingham
Directed by Krzysztof Lang

Paper Marriage is an attempt to cash in on a *Green Card*-style movie that trys to extract comedy from international relationships.

Alicja is a Polish immigrant who has one failed marriage of convenience behind her, as a doctor who met her in Warsaw ditches her on arrival in the UK. In search of self-improvement, she makes a paper contract with UK resident Aiden, played by ex-New Romantic Gary Kemp. Having tied the knot at Newcastle Civic Centre, she discovers that Aiden is in fact a conman who owes two thousand pounds to the local mob. The couple are based at a bed and breakfast run by Rita Tushingham who seems to be giving her version of the old radio landlady 'Mrs Mac', originally played by Molly Weir.

The plot is predictable - will the couple survive the pressures of the local mob and will a marriage of convenience turn into a true mating of souls? This is a slight comedy with attempts to emulate old Hollywood RomComs, particularly in the bedroom farce scenes in the bed and breakfast. The problem is that Alicja and Aiden are no Doris Day or Rock Hudson.

There are also some touches of reality. Alicja is exploited as a cleaner in offices opposite Newcastle Odeon. More concerning, she works as a hostess in a thinly disguised Grey's Club as a way of working off Aiden's debt to his corrupt boss. The outcome of the film is quite predictable as they ride out on a scooter across the Tyne Bridge.

In terms of location it's a Newcastle 'Pick and Mix'. As we cross the High Level Bridge the soundtrack is Metro FM. There is a sumptuous night shot of Grey Street, an ambush in the Bigg Market and a scene where Aiden hopelessly attempts to make burgers at the Quayside Sunday market.

In a film that generally went completely and perhaps understandably under the radar there are two wonderful local cameos. Aiden jams with a street musician who is of course the legendary Ray Stubbs one man blues band. The other cameo is Aiden in bed, not with Alicja, but with a copy of *Viz* comic - it is a mystery why Aiden and Alicja never turned up as a *Viz* comic strip themselves!

Finney (1994)

David Morrissey as Steven Finney
Melanie Hill as Lena Finney
Andy Serkis as Tom Finney
John Woodvine as Bobo Simpson
Directed by David Hayman

Finney is a television prequel to Mike Figgis's *Stormy Monday*. It is based around the origins of the Newcastle Jazz Club owner Steven Finney, played by Sting in the 1988 movie. Both movie and TV series were produced by Nigel Stafford-Clarke.

Steven Finney, who has one foot in jazz and one in organised crime, is played by David Morrissey, who had to acquire a Geordie accent and, it is said, learned to play the double bass. Having distanced himself from the family in London, Steven has to return to Newcastle, just like Jack Carter, in the wake of his father's murder. The three Finney children must find out why their father was murdered. Who did it? Was it rival family head Bobo Simpson? Will they protect the remaining empire in the North East?

The reading of the will sets up the plot up for the rest of the series. In a bizarre clause, Steven inherits a derelict cinema in Newcastle which, against all opposition, he will turn into a successful jazz club, despite a rhetorical question 'Does anybody in Newcastle want jazz?' The seismic shock is that his sister Lena has been left in charge of the criminal Finney empire, thereby disinheriting brother Tom, a vulnerable gambler and drug addict. The fallout from this situation makes for a grittily directed and scripted plot. Tom goes into lethal self-destruct mode, attempting to murder rival Bobo Simpson, Steven is reluctantly drawn from his jazz ambitions into a family gang war and Lena makes every Machiavellian move in the book.

Andy Serkis made *Finney* his last TV acting appearance before playing Gollums and gorillas on the big screen. His portrayal of an embittered manic sibling, who goes more out of control as the weeks go by, is a tour-de-force. For many, the main acting honours go to the Sunderland-born actress Melanie Hill. Her cold quest for revenge and justice for her father's unexplained murder creates a character who is truly the female equivalent of Jack Carter with a dash of old mother Kray. We witness two graphic interrogations at her hands - a naked rival male club owner is made to burn his clothes and incinerate a pile of his own slot machines in public gaze while she gloats on and the other interrogation involves the uncomfortable use

of a child's swing in a public park. The message is clear – DON'T mess with Lena Finney!

It was great fun for me to play the daughter of a gangster and particularly to hear so many Geordie accents. I love the accent and I love to hear it on television. It was good to portray a powerful woman as I rarely got parts like this and always seemed to be playing a sidekick. It seems to be getting better for getting good female roles and there are more female directors and writers now though there is still room for improvement! There was always talk of a sequel to Finney *which would feature two female leads including me, but of course it never happened - that's the nature of the business.*

Melanie Hill

There is an abundance of sharp humour and cinema homage. A mysterious hitman from London constantly tells people that he hates the North and that Newcastle is a filthy city, as he despatches a rival on Dunston Staiths. The same hitman pursues Finney in a Ghost Train in a fairground a la Hitchcock and is electrocuted à la Oddjob. Much of the series was filmed in Glasgow but there are glimpses of Central Station, Surtees Hotel, the Bridge Hotel, All Saints churchyard overlooking the Tyne Bridge and the ubiquitous Ray Stubbs again!

Despite being a compelling watch, *Finney* had the misfortune to be screened in direct opposition to Jimmy Nail's *Crocodile Shoes* series on BBC One - that really is the Geordie Mafia for you! Oh yes – there's a dodgy version of *Birdland* performed in Finney's new club.

Our Friends in the North (1996)

Christopher Eccleston as Nicky Hutchinson (9 episodes)
Mark Strong as Tosker Cox (9 episodes)
Gina McKee as Mary Cox (9 episodes)
Daniel Craig as Geordie Peacock (8 episodes)
Peter Vaughan as Felix Hutchinson (8 episodes)
David Bradley as Eddie Wells (8 episodes)
Freda Dowie as Florrie Hutchinson (7 episodes)
Alun Armstrong as Austin Donohue (5 episodes)
Malcolm McDowell as Benny Barrett (5 episodes)
Julian Fellowes as Claud Seabrook (3 episodes)
Charlie Hardwick as Paula Bennett (1 episode)

Directed by Simon Cellan Jones, Pedr James, Stuart Urban
Written by Peter Flannery

When *Our Friends in the North* came up in conversation with BBC Newcastle journalist Peg Alexander, she told me, 'Daniel Craig? Never mind about him jumping off trains and exploding buildings as 007, just give me him crossing the Tyne Bridge to the sound of Oasis - that's Daniel Craig for me.'

This is just one of the indelible images from what is the perfect storm of British television drama. Over nine episodes each set in a different year (1964, 1966, 1967, 1970, 1974, 1979, 1984, 1987 and 1995) we share the lives, loves, losses and changing fortunes of four North East friends and their families. Such is the power of writer Peter Flannery that we feel that we have actually lived these lives or at least part of them, and in a way we have. These four characters are supported by a fine repertory company which includes Alun Armstrong, Peter Vaughan, David Bradley, Julian Fellowes and Malcolm McDowell (in his first TV role). They find themselves performing in front of a revolving zoetrope of major historic events - ranging over three decades of government elections, industrial strife, and political corruption - all of which have a life-changing impact on their (and our) lives.

This is a saga of careers and ambitions with history being used as a locating device. Our four friends (the key characters) embrace political ambition, public relations, anarchy, photography, protection enforcement, council leadership, social mobility,

'Rachmanism' and union agitation. All of this unravels in front of a North East and Newcastle background, though Sunderland, London and Dartmoor were used as well.

In his *BFI TV Classics* book on the series, Michael Eaton describes the concluding episode nine (1995), as a perfect symmetry between location and character in the City of Newcastle. We see Tosker, now an entrepreneur on the deck of a floating nightclub, his teenage musical ambition sated by jamming with an 'Animals' tribute act. Nicky is racing after Mary, the Byker Wall behind him, and the Tyne Bridge behind her:

Geordie, once again abandoned, stomps off alone across the bridge, looking down to see Tosker playing with his grandchildren on the deck of his boat. On the North bank of the Tyne, Mary and Nicky have perhaps been offered another stab at happiness tomorrow. On the South side, Tosker seems to have achieved happiness today.

Our Friends in the North (BFI TV Classics)

Our Friends in the North was never intended for television consumption. Peter Flannery wrote it as a 'state of the nation' stage play in 1981 when he was writer in residence at the Royal Shakespeare Company. Championed by the BBC's Michael Wearing, who against all odds saw its television potential. Flannery and what became an ever-evolving series from the original, were shunted for years like rolling stock on the rail network that is known as the BBC commissioning system. It emerged gleaming on BBC Two screens with an unprecedented budget of at least seven million pounds.

I interviewed Peter Flannery, who has also successfully dramatised *George Gently*, in Northumberland in February 2016:

When you were growing up in Jarrow what first impression did Newcastle have on you?

Well you have to remember we are talking about early to mid-sixties, therefore transport was a massive issue, Newcastle was a hard place to get to. The bus would take up to an hour. It was like going to somewhere like Paris now, not that it looked anything like Paris when you got there! I didn't start coming to Newcastle until I was in my early to mid-teens. Me and a mate I used to go to town and we decided we wanted to be mods. We used to roll up on the No. 18 bus, with limited funds and we'd get our hair cut - a complete waste of money to do this every week! We used to go to shops such as 'Clobber' which was filthy, this was before the clean up where the buildings on Grey Street weren't grey they were black with pollution, the Cathedral was also black, the Tyne had far fewer bridges. In one of the shops on the Bigg Market I saw a copy of *Private Eye* in the window and started buying it for a shilling and read it on the way home which took another bloody hour!

In short, it was an exotic place for me, I never went to any shows or anything of that nature. I think the first show I ever went to was in Jesmond at the Old Flora Robson Playhouse in the late sixties, I would have gone straight from school. The very first thing I saw in the theatre was *Under Milk Wood*, hardly a play at all, it was just people sitting on stools. I also saw *Merchant of Venice* at that same theatre which is only goes to show I didn't see much live theatre. I probably saw a hundred to a hundred and fifty films and five thousand TV dramas before I went to the theatre - but Newcastle itself meant an exotic location and it seemed strange and big - Jarrow was such a small place. I didn't even live in Jarrow, I lived on an over-spill estate called Primrose, in a tiny little cul-de-sac in prefabs surrounded by land that had been earmarked for development. Basically it was a tip and it was still a tip when I left, it's nice now though. It was a great place to play and have adventures with open sewer pipes, ponds, and so we imported all of our television programmes on to those locations. Played endless games of *Lone Ranger* and such like.

Your grandfather was in the Jarrow March and that was eighty years ago this year. I remember you said that your father's political inertia annoyed you.

The first question I'm asked about *Our Friends in the North* was why am I so fired up about social and political change, and why were my father and my mother utterly cynical about it?

One of the things they would refer to is the Jarrow March and the fact that those men were cheated and treated so badly and nothing appeared to change. Hitler changed it, he changed the North East, he got them back to work but the British government did nothing, and that sense of betrayal stayed with him all his life. He must have only been seventeen, he didn't march, his father did. That sense of betrayal went into my dad's life and could easily have gone into mine, except of course someone let me spend eight million pounds making a television show about it.

Your original stage play plot ended in the year 1979. A key figure is Austin Donohue (Jim Broadbent/Alun Armstrong) based on T. Dan Smith - 'Mr Newcastle' whose vision ultimately landed him in prison.

Well I still find Dan a bit of a mystery. I did spend a lot of time with him from when I started writing *Our Friends in the North* in 1980. A journalist gave me Dan's number and I rang him and just said I would like to write a play. I was working for the RSC who commissioned me - I could write about anything I wanted and I kind of wanted to write about what happened up here. He agreed to meet me straight away. He said 'there could be a play of Shakespearian proportions here' and of course we know who he saw as the Shakespearian hero. I didn't get to know Smith well, but I did spend a lot of time with him - he was very good at acting a part and being who he wanted to be. He was so clever and so articulate that he tied me up in knots. I ended coming to my own conclusions about the character I wanted to write about. You could never pin him down about where the money went and why exactly he did it. He was completely innocent as far as he was concerned. He kept pointing out that he was never ever found guilty of anything and he was tried four times and was acquitted three times. He pleaded guilty the fourth time because he ran out of energy and had a bad heart so he gave in. But he always claimed he was never found guilty, and everything he did was in the public's interest. He thought it all worked entirely to benefit of poor people. They got houses, roads, they got infrastructure. But when you said to him 'But the houses fell down Dan', he would blame somebody else. He would blame Poulson, or he would blame the government. He would say he built high density because the government wouldn't release land for us to build low density. And that was true. They were protecting the green belt.

Sometimes he was funny and you would say 'Dan look at the unfinished motorways. What you were trying to do? building a strangulating necklace of roads around the city centre and we are left with this absurd one way system which doesn't work?' And he would say 'Have you ever been to Venice? You can't help but notice a tight ring of canals around the city centre' and I would say 'Yes, I know and we are the Venice of the North and all that, but can I just tell you something. I never heard anybody jump into a gondola in Newcastle and say 'Just drive me around the Ring Road!' I think that was the only time there was no come back from him. But I liked him and I liked his expansiveness, I liked the fact that he had been so active in promoting the arts with the Northern Arts Council, and I liked his very early ideas on federalism and regionalism. He always said the North East would prosper better in a federal Europe.

It took fourteen years to appear on TV.

The fourteen years was mainly them not me. I used the fourteen years to the profit of the show in the end because I was able to write about the main characters as middle aged people when *I* was middle aged. I created the characters when I was twenty-eight and finished their stories when I was forty-four - you don't normally get a chance to do that. It's not a great way to earn a living but it's a great way to write something.

As the years passed did you find yourself writing more about the personalities than the politics?

I think there was a massive change between the play and the television version. The play is far more political and far less interested in human beings. At twenty-eight years old I was more interested in the politics than the humanity of things. I think I just got a bit older and I had the birth of my daughter. This completely changed my view of the world - it happened almost overnight and everything I had written before the birth of my daughter in 1985 is different. So I wrote the first versions of the TV show in 1985, by the time I was asked to write it again in 1989 I was just a different bloke. I'd written *Singer* in the meantime which was still political and a very emotional piece, I never went back to writing from the outside-in, I always stay inside-out. It's because your children are growing up and your parents growing old and dying, you can write all about that and the state of the world, at the same time. I have never really gone back from that, but it got me an audience, a massive audience. That's why I often describe it as 'posh soap opera', I'm not trying to disparage it. I'm just saying it engages with people on a very basic human and emotional level, as well as politically. I think everything I have written since then has been intended to go about things the same way.

During the limbo of the commission system, is it true that the BBC suggested fictionalising the setting from England to 'Albion'?

They wanted it set in Albion or similar, as they thought they would get around all sorts of legal problems such as defamations, slanders and libel, if it was from somewhere called Albion rather than in real place like England. This was part of a conversation with a lawyer who threatened to resign if the BBC put *Our Friends in the North* into production, he said it was so defamatory of almost everybody. It was the police he was particularly worried about, he wasn't too worried about T. Dan Smith and Poulson because they had all gone to prison. He accepted that I couldn't lose a man his reputation if he had been found guilty of corruption.

You even encountered opposition even referring to the North.

Politics in drama was out at the time, it had been out for quite some time - too expensive, too political, too 'northern'. The northern thing didn't come from lawyers, it came from a BBC executive who said 'does it have to have north in the title and does it have to be about the labour party?' I said what is the problem with either of those things? His reply was he didn't want 'losers' on his channel!

I still think there is a perception that when people say 'the North' in BBC terms, they think its Salford.

When I went to Manchester University as an eighteen year old, as far as I was concerned I was going south. When I first heard the accents on *The Likely Lads* I was still living up here. I had no idea where they were supposed to be from, they weren't Geordie accents as far as I was concerned.

That's very interesting I've got records of audience reaction from the BBC, and a lot people said 'why do we have to watch these 'Midlanders'?'

They didn't want to do Geordie accents, probably because they would be frightened that nobody would understand any of it. I remember watching it thinking what bit of the North East is this? I'm not taking anything away from *The Likely Lads* as I loved it, but I was just baffled by it. It was witty and it was sardonic.

Without me realising it, it was also capturing the rise of the aspirational working class and the conflicts there in. That was all very interesting - it dramatised it and articulated it. Basically I liked it because of the wit.

A lot of people fondly remember When the Boat Comes In.

It was probably very influential on me, again without me realising I was absorbing it. It was an epic and guess what I ended up writing?

After all the battles of development you then turn this seven million pound juggernaut around because you didn't like how episode one had turned out.

It was exactly as I had written it, but just not very well filmed and we parted company with the director. We decided to reshoot episode one and then the producers actually suggested that this would be a perfect opportunity for us to rewrite it if we would like to. I said 'so you mean we could completely re-shoot episode one?' - so that's what we did. I wrote it in bigger, brighter colours with completely different action, starting the story in completely different parts in their lives. The actors went mad, as you can imagine. It was re-shot during their holiday!

But you find there were certain scenes we couldn't reshoot, the demolition scene where Geordie is sitting on a child's swing - a house is being demolished behind him and he goes to talk to Eddy about it afterwards. We had to keep that because we couldn't remount it, it would have been too expensive. In his hand he's got a gift-wrapped football which he is taking to the christening to give to Tosker and Mary's baby. So I had to change that into a birthday present for Nicky - and that's what the whole scene becomes about this ball he has bought for Nicky - they have been giving it to each other on their birthdays all their lives. So certain things like that we had to keep and just work around them.

What us your favourite scene visually?

It's Nicky looking down that night when he is in despair, he sees Austin is coming out of the Guild Hall onto the Quayside, they catch each other up and they go for a walk. It's the winter of the electricity strikes and he's about to be arrested. Nicky doesn't know what to do anymore. He's lost his relationship with his family, he's lost Mary and he's lost Austin Donohue. It's a very bleak scene and it's night, but it's *that* bridge again.

There's also the iconic picture of the bridge with Geordie walking across and looking down at his old mate Tosker who is now a happy granddad, sitting on the boat playing with his grandchildren. I guess for me it's always the bridge.

Did you tailor specific scenes to the location, for instance where Geordie is talking to Sean opposite the Tuxedo Princess?

I knew we were using the boat so I knew exactly where that was going to be. Obviously, in the earlier scripts (some of which were written in the early eighties) a lot of it wasn't even built then. I think much of the quayside didn't exist, so you will find there are no scenes set on the quayside for that reason. I think it has much less of a sense of place in the early scenes and much more of one as it opens out in the nineties.

Twenty years on, where have you arrived now?

I'm still optimistic about, and believe in political change. I haven't altered my view on that. I think it gets harder and harder and I don't think we live in the small world that I started writing about. We now live in a massive world and new doors of corruption keep opening up to us that we never believed existed. If it's not banking, it's sport and there is some cause for becoming more disillusioned and unhappy. But because I believe in the fundamental good nature of ordinary people, I will go on writing about that. But none of it will be made.

If you went to the BBC with this now ?

Not a chance in hell! Every time I write anything that goes outside the genre like *George Gently*, it doesn't get made. I have no more time to spend writing scripts that don't get made. The difference is with *Our Friends in the North*, I was prepared to go on year after year - because I was thirty and they (the BBC execs) were sixty and dying off, but now *I'm* sixty-four and *they* are thirty. I have to do what I want to do now and I don't think it's *Our Friends in the North*. I have the ambition but I don't think they have.

Not many realise the origin of the title *Our Friends in the North*. Unfortunately, it is not a reference to Newcastle or the region. It is in fact a term used by BP oil in South Africa as their reference to *their* 'friends in the North' - the regime in Rhodesia. The Rhodesian plot (in the play) was completely exorcised from the television series.

Two threads have always fascinated me. The first is the role of high rise flats ensuing from the Austin Donohue plot line. Willow Lane flats are first occupied by the hopeful Mary and Tosker, then as the dampness encroaches they become the object of a campaign led by Mary and Eddie Wells. By 1974, Nicky is actually occupying Mary and Tosker's old flat, five years later we see them demolished on local television. Ironically, Tosker begins to rent out suspect property as flats before the stock market crash wipes him out. Property, its aspirations polarised into corrupt proceedings, runs like a social barometer through the series.

The second thread is music. The soundtrack choice is key to this 'posh soap opera.' In the 60s, Tosker brandishes his guitar as a short cut to women and money. Geordie plays The Animals *We gotta get outta this place* in one of the Machiavellian Benny Barratt's Soho clip joints. This song was originally written for the Righteous Brothers but was hijacked by The Animals as an anthem for escape - not just from Newcastle - from anywhere. The song returns in episode nine, played by an Animals tribute act on board Tosker's pleasure boat. In a 1980s' episode, we hear *Two Tribes* by Frankie Goes to Hollywood, perhaps a reflection of *The Tube* TV show - which turned Newcastle into the capital of cool because

The Tube discovered the band. Finally, *that* scene of Geordie Peacock stumbling across the bridge of sighs or dreams to the sound of Oasis. *Don't Look Back in Anger* charted during the week of episode nine's transmission - pure coincidence, a wet dream for any record promotional department...

Peter Flannery has admitted that Mary, Tosker, Geordie and Nicky were all aspects of himself. Where are the friends now? Is Mary a Labour peer? Is Geordie still alive? Is Nicky overseeing a retrospective of his collected photographic works at the Side Gallery? Is Tosker perhaps CEO of Cox Quayside Holdings? Look forward in anger!

Only one member of the cast of four has returned to a North East dramatic scene. Gina McKee played Pauline Pearson in the quirky Tyneside comedy *Hebburn* from 2012 to 2013.

Quayside (January-May 1997)

Seventeen episodes
Co-devised by Matthew Robinson and Brian B. Thompson
Cast included Glenn McCrory, Joe Caffrey, Bob Smeaton, Yvette Rowland
Directors included Tom Hooper

When *Coronation Street* brought Northern working class life to the small screen, Tyne Tees Television, based in an old furniture warehouse on City Road, didn't initially transmit Britain's first and greatest soap in the region. The reasons why they chose not to have never been clear, but we seem to have been paying for it ever since. Despite claims made in the name of *Byker Grove* and *Our Friends in the North*, there has never been a successful Tyneside-based soap drama. One reason may be found with Corrie's creator Tony Warren who was initially inspired by the strong female role models that surrounded him in Manchester. Perhaps the fact that North East society is traditionally male and macho in its stance it therefore doesn't lend itself to weekly drama played out in streets and cul-de-sacs.

The nearest challenger to the soap stakes was the ill-fated Zenith North production for Tyne Tees Television, *Quayside*.

Simon Heath was the serial's story editor and part script writer:

This was a regional drama, taking advantage of a weekly 'opt-out' slot from the ITV Network. It wasn't a family soap, it was about entrepreneurial Geordies set on a regenerating Quayside amongst a vibrant nightclub scene. Basically we had a young cast, little time and little money, so we had no time to develop, which is what a successful soap really needs.

The executive producer was Matthew Robinson who pioneered/produced both *Byker Grove* and *Eastenders*. Angling around a TV climate of 'youthful soaps' he announced in the *Journal* on October 14th 1996 that:

'This is a feel-good factor soap which reflects the amazing vibrancy of the area. There will be no 'issues', no gloom and no doom.'

The team behind *Quayside* were in fact the same who had

nurtured the success of *Byker Grove* for Zenith North. Joining Simon Heath and Matthew Robinson, as series co-deviser, and writer of seven episodes, was the most prolific *Byker Grove* writer Brian B. Thompson:

Great cast, great crew and a great chance to make another long running show in the North East. What could possibly go wrong?

Zenith North were keen to get another hit and persuaded Tyne Tees Television into using the local opt out slot and its tiny budget for a soap - something which had never been done before. It was an opportunity we had to take but, with little time available, it was a classic case of trying to run before we could walk. The Quayside's mixture of new flats, bars and offices made it a great place to see our characters at work and play, and with the Tyne bridges looming above, it was the perfect location.

Okay, I'll come clean, I wrote nine of the seventeen episodes of *Quayside*. (Not much about it on IMDb, I wonder why?!). I note from the script that shooting began on 21 October 1996 and it went out on January 7 1997. To everyone's great credit, it was made on time and on budget.

Any problems with the final show were magnified by the anticipation. It was an ultra-low budget regional soap and as such was never likely to win a BAFTA, but it was in the local press as 'We'll take on *EastEnders*'. That was always going to be difficult, not just because of our resources but because it takes time to build that sort of familiarity with characters. Plus, it was more of a cheap and cheerful *Neighbours* than a grittier ensemble piece a la Albert Square.

Not great drama then, but let's dig out some positives. It was Newcastle's first and only soap and, you could argue, the city's first post-industrial TV drama. Newcastle's industrial heritage was central to just about every show from *When the Boat Comes In* through to *The Likely Lads* and still casting a long, moody shadow over *Spender*. In *Quayside* the two main characters (Mal and Cat) were firmly in the new Newcastle, part of the service industries like everyone else. The image of the Tyne Bridge, which had so often been associated with the region's twin bedfellows of pride and sorrow, was all about romance and partying in *Quayside* – a connection that continues to this day in *Geordie Shore*. In fact, in many ways party girl Nicole from *Quayside* was the teen mum begetter of Vicky Pattison.

Too little in terms of time and budget conspired to end *Quayside* in under six months and its more risible qualities found their way into a canon of *Quayside* jokes on the local comedy circuit. Despite claims of a forty per cent audience share, *Quayside* was axed after disappointing viewing figures.

The cast had included ex-professional boxer Glenn McCrory and future Grammy winner, documentary maker Bob Smeaton. Series director Tom Hooper would win an academy award as director of *The King's Speech*.

The region has given great acting talent to the soaps - Charlie Hardwick to *Emmerdale* and Melanie Hill to *Coronation Street*. We can still hope that a successful soap opera may yet come that focuses on life in Newcastle and the area, not just in terms of kudos and tourism, but for the film and television industry itself. One of the country's leading location managers, Gareth Williams, whose talents have been seen in productions ranging from *Wire In The Blood* to *Wolfblood* makes an important point:

A successful soap in the region would mean regular employment and stability for local cast and crews. It would also contribute to the establishment of a permanent rather than an itinerant film and television production base, Think about it, Hollyoaks *maintains six crews full time in that region year in and year out.*

Brian B. Thompson has pointed out, with his tongue slightly in his cheek, that *Quayside* is not found on many CVs.

Newcastle's Quayside, 2014.

Purely Belter (2000)

Chris Beattie as Gerry McCarten
Greg McLane as Sewell
Charlie Hardwick as Mrs McCarten
Tim Healey as Mr McCarten
Also starring Roy Hudd and Kevin Whately
Directed by Mark Herman

Film dramas about sport have one major problem. To reach the
widest audience they have to attempt to preach to the unconverted.
In recent years there has been a key change in successful films of
this type - big screen documentaries or dramas about racing drivers
and golfers.

When it comes to rugby and football there has been a chequered
past, examples are *This Sporting Life*, *Fever Pitch*, *When Saturday
Comes* and *Escape to Victory*. It is inevitable that Newcastle's St
James's Park should provide a backdrop to two very different sets
of ambitions relating to football and the fortunes of Newcastle
United.

Purely Belter (2000) is the story of two young, underprivileged,
working class Newcastle United fans, Gerry (Chris Beattie) and
Sewell (Greg McLane) who literally beg, steal and borrow to raise
enough money to buy a coveted season ticket for the match.
Director Mark Herman adapted an original story by local author
Jonathan Tulloch. Herman had already successfully adapted and
directed *Little Voice* and *Brassed Off* for the screen. He was
fascinated by the humour, resourcefulness and pathos that emerged
from an ostensibly unattractive story and its capacity to draw you
in to the boys' flawed world.

*The two main characters Gerry and Sewell, were brilliantly drawn,
at the same time very funny and very tragic, and the world they
inhabited appealed to the filmmaker in me...most importantly of
all, this was the story about people, not the people's game.*

*Filming in Tyneside in November was always going to be hard
work, short days and brass monkeys, but being in a city that knows
how to have a good time, I don't think anyone really noticed.*
from *Purely Belter* (*Film 4 Books*) by Mark Herman

The film was originally titled *Season Ticket*, the title of the book, then *Pure Belter* and finally *Purely Belter*, which was thought to best translate to a wider audience. The cast is an interesting mixture. The two young leads had little or no on screen experience. As the story unfolds over the four seasons of the year, Gerry and Sewell interact with the members of their respective dysfunctional families. Sewell has a Geordie granddad with Alzheimer's played by veteran Roy Hudd. Gerry's absentee abusive father is Tim Healy and his bullying teacher is his *Auf Wiedersehen Pet* sidekick Kevin Whately.

It is a tribute to director Herman that the chemistry between the untried Chris Beattie and Greg McLane is so natural, nearly improvised, demonstrating that more theatrically trained actors might have jeopardised the mixture of gritty hardship and humour. Through the course of the film we follow them collecting scrap, conning the public with an overpriced 'pound for the guy' scheme, avoiding the bribes of a social worker and even faking blindness to extract sympathy and money from passers-by. There are two high points of humour, when they unknowingly steal Alan Shearer's car and debate his appalling taste in music from the cassettes found in

the glove compartment. Perfectly framed in another scene by the High Level Bridge, the two boys discuss the merits of reselling articles stolen from 'Everything's A Pound' - can they in fact be sold for more than that?.

The signature performance in the film is that of Gerry's mother, Mrs McCarten portrayed by actress Charlie Hardwick. Plagued by ill-health, Gerry's mother is constantly fighting to survive violent abuse from her husband and always seems to be on the jaws of defeat:

When I think of the Mam in *Purely Belter*, my stomach tenses, my breathing becomes shallow and my eyes feel slow and narrowed - characters remain in your cell memory you know. She's a woman who has had the living daylights crushed out of her and she is crouched, in 'flight' mode like an animal waiting for the next 'attack'. She cannot gain control of her situation or protect her children. As the film progresses and their circumstances worsen through the seasons she gets more and more exhausted and ill, more and more crushed, until she physically can't draw breath.

Mark Herman was very clear about the Mam's downward trajectory and we plotted her deterioration in detail, both mentally and physically. The costume and make-up designers were crucial in this discussion, the Mam slowly changes from colour to black and

white in pallor and apparel. We planned even hair-growth meticulously. I love this collaborative approach to character.

Mark wanted there to be hope at the end of the film, she is given the chance to breathe again following the death of the man who was systematically destroying her and her family. She's released from her living hell and starting to breathe with both lungs.

Mark was a man of few words as a director, if he was happy with the shots and the scenes - he moved on. If there was something that he wanted us to try differently, he came on set and had a quiet conversation, and suggested a different thought or movement. This was always concise and precise, encouraging a tiny change in performance or motivation, not dictating a pre-conceived idea. I think he trusted the actors he had cast, and we trusted that if he wasn't happy he would not move on. This rarely happened. The atmosphere on set was concentrated and focussed and very clear. It was an intense role but a great pleasure to work with Mark. We were safe in his hands.

Charlie Hardwick

Gerry and Sewell's scams become more outrageous, culminating in a farcical bank robbery where Grey Street's Theatre Royal effectively doubles as a bank entrance. There is an irony that the denouement sees the boys doing community service for their bank crime. It is that punishment that will earn them the ultimate access to St James's Park that they have spent four seasons of petty crime trying to achieve. In some quarters Mark Herman's film was criticised for its brand of feel-good socialism. *Purely Belter* in fact makes a grimly humorous point - that for many, including Sewell and Gerry, what is called the 'People's Game' is unobtainable.

Once again Newcastle provides a perfect visual space for our two protagonists to operate in. There are stunning views of the bridges from Byker and also of the Tyne Bridge and the Central Bar when Gerry searches for his father to the sound of the Prodigy's *Firestarter*. The Get Carter car park provides, yet again, another location where they are reprimanded by a security guard. The ultimate irony - both lead actors were Sunderland supporters.

Purely Belter also suffered from being released in the same year as *Billy Elliott* - North East familiarity may have bred contempt for blinkered distributors.

Gabriel and Me (2001)

Iain Glen as Dad
David Bradley as Grandad
Sean Landless as Jimmy
Rosie Rowell as Mam
Billy Connolly as Gabriel
Ian Cullen as Ridley
Directed by Udayan Prasad
Screenplay by Lee Hall (Based on *I love You Jimmy Spud*)

Gabriel and Me tells the story of Jimmy Spud, an eleven year old who lives with his parents in the Byker Wall. His father is terminally ill and, as an unemployed welder, has unsuccessfully attempted to supplement the family income with painting and sketching. There are constant tensions between his father and mother and also the powerful figure of Jimmy's grandfather, a socialist and former dockside crane operator, portrayed by David Bradley (Eddie Wells of *Our Friends in the North*).

In a touching sequence Jimmy hides in the control box of his grandfather's old crane (located in his grandfather's memory) within sight of the Neptune Yard and the home of the *Mauretania*. There are some light-hearted exchanges over television viewing habits - brutish father, philosphical grandfather and encumbered mother arguing over the merits of Channel Four versus *Blind Date* and whether they should watch what Jimmy's father describes as Bolshoi bollocks!

This rites of passage story is driven by loner Jimmy's recurring early memory of flying through the air like an angel and he sets out to become one, in an effort to save his father.

Surrealistically, he finds himself actually serving an angel apprenticeship mentored by none other than the Angel Gabriel himself, played by Billy Connolly.

Some critics wrote that they couldn't decide whether it was Billy Connolly as Gabriel or Gabriel as Billy Connolly!

In this gentle film there are touching moments, Jimmy playing trumpet for his hospitalised father, releasing the pigeons from his grandfather's lofts and making a spectacular dive from a shipyard crane. The encounters with Gabriel are given real poignancy as the two figures meet in cavernous dry docks. As to whether he achieves his ambition, well, I'm not issuing any spoilers.

It's interesting that *Gabriel and Me* is one of the few dramas that is set in the extraordinary Byker Wall, the multi-coloured screen of humanity that replaced the slum dwellings of the Byker community.

Gabriel and Me is really about rising above where you are, literally or metaphorically. It's about overcoming non-communication between a father and son in a North East setting, which includes the Freeman Hospital and a reasonably calm Roker Pier. Play/screenplay writer Lee Hall was less than enthusiastic about the results:

I grew up watching Byker change. It's where my Grandparents grew up and so I watched it all happen. Ralph Erskine's work is quite extraordinary. It's safe to say the feelings of people were quite ambivalent to it, but I felt it was an interesting place to film. The whole affair was completely botched for me. I introduced the director to the area showed him around Walker and Byker where I wanted the film to be set, but he rewrote the film himself and I left the project. I have never seen the film so I have no idea what he did.

Lee Hall

Left: *Long before they met again in* Game of Thrones, *Iain Glen with David Bradley.*

The One and Only (2002)

Justine Waddell as Stevie
Richard Roxburgh as Neil
Jonathon Cake as Andrea/Sonny
Patsy Kensit as Stella
Michael Hodgson as Stan
Directed by Simon Cellan-Jones
Adapted by Peter Flannery From *Den Eneste Den*

The One and Only was a romantic comedy that promised, at last, to deliver Newcastle from its roots in the stereotypical gritty gangster genre. Adapted from the Danish box office hit *Den Eneste Den* by Peter Flannery, it seems perfect for the noughties. Neil is a kitchen fitter for whom it's love at first sight when he delivers a kitchen to Stevie. However, a number of problems stand in the way of true love. Neil is in a childless marriage with Jenny and they are adopting an African girl in an effort to save their relationship. Stevie, married to an adulterous football player, has just discovered that she is pregnant. Will Stevie and Neil ever end up together? Fate plays a brutal and unexpected card when Jenny is killed in a freak traffic accident, but the path of unintended true love still doesn't run smoothly for the rest of the film.

There are many good moments in Flannery's script, some reflecting the background regeneration of Newcastle's post-industrial Quayside, and life and its social pressures in a changing urban landscape. A favourite scene is a debate between Neil and Stan as they sit in their van opposite the nearly completed Baltic Centre for Contemporary Art. There follows a debate on the definition of art - is real art Titian's 'fat lasses' or what looks like 'Ikea furniture nailed to the floor?'

The film failed to deliver its initial promise, despite being visually sumptuous. The main problem was the total lack of chemistry between actors Richard Roxburgh and Justine Waddell. There is in fact far more chemistry in the sub-plot involving Michael Hodgson and Patsy Kensit as Stan and Stella, particularly when they give new meaning to the expression 'Supermarket Sweep'.

Critics rounded on the variations in Geordie accents from lead cast members and Patsy Kensit was also the subject of some unfortunate publicity about her size. It is alleged that the film only

took £1,200 pounds at the box office in the North East. The film was a reunion of the writer of *Our Friends in the North* - Peter Flannery and director, Simon Cellan Jones.

The One and Only was taken from the Dutch film. The original was funny and witty so we thought 'how about a Geordie version of it?' The producer said 'just take the story and the characters and do want you want with it, but set it on Tyneside'. I immediately wanted to write about a footballer which is not in the original version.

So I thought here is Newcastle now with rich and poor, there is development on the Quayside, let's make it about that and let's set it there. The director went further than that, he's made a kind of love film to Newcastle which wasn't quite what I had in mind. He did it a little too much for me. It's a bit like *Stormy Monday* except more romantic and again he makes it look a sexy place, but it's also a funny place and slightly more real than *Stormy Monday*. But it is about change, and it has something to say. It's about who you love and about finding happiness. I would have liked (and this is not a complaint about the actress who is a wonderful actress) a down to earth Geordie actress playing that part and finding her love in the Geordie kitchen man. But we ended up with an Australian playing the kitchen man and a South African playing the Geordie girl and I think we lost something.

I love Geordies and I love their 'down to earthism' - it's where I come from and it's my family, but the film is about change and the mistrust of change.

Peter Flannery

Whatever its reception, the film is visually stunning and was welcomed with open arms by Newcastle City Council. The Quayside glows, every window seems to have a river view and there is an amazing scene where Neil dances with his adopted daughter on a rooftop near the Tyne Bridge.

Christine Llewellyn-Reeve, Location Manager, *The One and Only*:

I felt real joy of being given the brief that Newcastle should be shown as a city of resurgence and regeneration, comparable with New York, Sydney and Paris. This was the first time I was being asked to show the region, and specifically Newcastle and Gateshead, in this positive way rather than constantly being asked to re-create the type-cast and out of date image of what we used to call 'Cobbles, Flat Caps and Whippet Handbags'. I remember the look of wonderment on the face of the then Gateshead Council Press Officer at the end of a preliminary planning meeting with all departments regarding filming on the yet unfinished Millennium Bridge and equally unfinished Baltic Flour Mill as he asked 'Let me get this right, you want to promote Gateshead and Newcastle as comparable with the great European Cities, full of energy, hope and fantastic architecture?' 'Yes' we said. 'So' he went on. 'What you are basically offering us is a three million pound promotional film that will be seen nationally and hopefully internationally at no cost to ourselves?' 'Yes' we said. Need I say that he shook our hands!

We had a technical 'recce' before making the film, we stood on the Gateshead Millennium Bridge to work out how to create the shot (involving a crane on a barge), of the two potential lovers standing in the middle of the bridge. The bridge was unfinished and not yet open to the public. We donned all the safety gear required and made our way to the centre of the bridge with the construction engineers and PR Team. Needless to say, the recce took place on a day when the North East was being battered by terrible gale force winds. As locals will know, the bridge is designed to 'bounce' slightly with each footfall or bicycle crossing. The wind increased the effect drastically. We hung on to the safety rails and had to shout above the noise of the wind! In the end we all had to give up and continue the discussion in a safe indoor office. What a privilege though, to be allowed onto the bridge with those that were building it well before it opened. We got the shot, quite an achievement, with those in the film industry still scratching their heads and wondering how we got that particular camera move. Again, the cooperation we received from both sides of the River was superb … permissions for filming on bridges is quite complex, and as usual everyone came up trumps.

Just before principal filming started, I stood on the Gateshead Millennium Bridge, right in the centre with Richard Roxbrough. He had wanted to check it out prior to the scene being shot. I have to admit I hadn't realised just how famous he was, but I did know he was Australian. I was delighted when he said the view reminded him of Sydney and he felt at home! I felt I had kept my promise to the film and the councils.

We got outstanding support from Gateshead Council in the tricky location requirement to feature the Baltic heavily. The construction company responsible for the development work were unstinting in their support. They were up against tight deadlines and I can only imagine what they might have thought when asked officially to help us in whatever way they could to achieve what we needed. In the script the building was not under construction. There were several scenes when the main character just sat in his car on the Newcastle Quayside, admiring it. We therefore had to find a way of achieving not just what appeared to be an untouched building, but also to deal with the problem of continuity. We filmed over eight weeks during which time the Baltic looked constantly different. Scaffolding on one side, then on the other, the crane in different positions, etc.

The interior of the building was virtually an empty shell with temporary scaffolding and wood floors and staircases. The director wanted to play the end scene, the happy wedding reception on the top floor of the Baltic, which in real life was planned to be a penthouse restaurant. The only way to get up there to see what state it was in, and might be in by the end of the shoot, was for me to go up with the chief construction manager via the only lift, which was the construction lift. This consisted of an outside metal grid cage. Hard hats, steel capped boots, hi-viz jackets all required. Not easy to get anything that fitted when I think I was just about the only woman on site. Now, I am not good even going up a ladder. I made this journey several times over the weeks, attempting to enjoy the amazing views but tightly holding on to the arm of the poor construction manager each time. I may have shut my eyes but who was to know under all that protective clothing. The interior, as you went up was a hive of activity, with dust, pipes, cables, scaffolding, slatted floors that allowed you to see right down through all the floors, until we got to the top. You felt you were witnessing a medieval cathedral under construction. The 'restaurant' at this point was just a metal framed shell. No windows, no floor, the beginnings of a basic roof but fantastic views. Against all the odds, the construction company and our Art Department managed to turn it into what appears to be a wedding venue. Fortunately the windows were installed (but only just) and a more solid roof, but a few days before the shoot the builders simply couldn't put a floor in place. The art department therefore laid a temporary floor. They disguised the ceiling with silver drapes, and imported all the tables, chairs, cakes, flowers etc to the top floor using nothing but the one exterior lift. All the lamps and equipment, cast and crew, including at least forty extras and a band, had to get to the location in the same way! Getting the right

CHRISTINE LLEWELLYN-REEVE

Above: *A long way down during the filming of* The One and Only. Below: *The top of the Baltic in 'disguise'.*

CHRISTINE LLEWELLYN-REEVE

115

electrical power up was another challenge. The construction company yet again, changed the scaffolding to a different corner of the building so it was not in shot and to ensure nothing would obscure the amazing views of Newcastle, Gateshead, the bridges and the river. They also stopped any work during filming that would be a problem for sound. We spent a happy, if nerve-racking three days prepping, filming and de-rigging up with the Gods in the clouds. The weather held and the results are great. I am one of the few people privileged to have seen the view from the now lovely ladies toilets while standing in the open air on a scaffolding platform. I would like to add that the building work finished on schedule!

The support and planning of the police, organising a speeding van sequence through the main streets of Newcastle City Centre was amazing. Planned on a Sunday, with a route that took in the Quayside, Mosley Street, Pilgrim Street and screamed to a halt at Central Station, there was another moment of traffic power, when

The 'Cheese Wedge' or Phoenix House could double as Paris, New York or London

116

CHRISTINE LLEWELLYN-REEVE

myself and the police officers assigned to us manually operated the relevant traffic lights on some on the busiest crossroads in Newcastle to stop traffic and allow our cars through safely! The sequence included spinning the van by the Guildhall at the bottom of The Side, then still open to traffic. The special effects company used a huge wooden circular platform on wheels onto which the van was placed and manually 'spun' with a camera inside and outside. We planned this around the Sunday Market where the Quayside road was already shut, and we managed the whole sequence without any additional road closures! It was achieved in one morning. Again, many salutes to the Highways Department and the Newcastle Police who planned it like a military operation!

We filmed all night at the corner of Queen Street opposite the Akenside Pub, under the Tyne Bridge in the area we always called 'The Cheese Wedge' due to the triangular shape of the wonderful apartment block under the Tyne Bridge. Patsy Kensit and Donna Air joined the real Tyneside late night revellers, sitting on the corner doorstep of the apartment building fictionally absolutely plastered, putting the world to rights while waiting for a lift home from Donna's footballer husband in a bright red Ferrari. I think we lit most of the area! Hours of prep lighting up the Guildhall exterior, the apartment building and the bottom of The Side, with the Akenside Pub offering refuge and green rooms. We needed them! The main hazard wasn't the interested pub crawling hoards, but the seagulls and Kittiwakes depositing unwanted gifts on our heads as they roosted overnight!

Wire in the Blood (2002-2008)

Robson Green as Tony Hill
Written by Val McDermid
Coastal Productions for ITV

The fictionalising of the Newcastle area has played a major part in television drama. Audiences constantly search for places they can identify in everything from Cookson dramas to the amazing exploits of *Supergran*, which was filmed by Tyne Tees Television in Tynemouth and the village of Earsdon.

When it comes to the solving of unspeakable crimes by flawed detectives the area has really come into its own. Val McDermid's creation, Tony Hill was brought to life by Robson Green as a clinical psychologist whose ability to tap into the dark side helps him to apprehend serial killers. In *Wire in the Blood*, Hill operates in the fictionalised grim, Northern industrial city of Bradfield. Bradfield is in a way 'every city' where the most heinous crimes are committed.

Coastal Productions, based on the Quayside, decided to use Newcastle as the basis of Bradfield. There was an irony in the fact that yesterday's shipyards and former sites of industrial prosperity would get a new lease of life as dramatic backdrops to McDermid's creation. Prior to becoming location manager for the most successful CBBC production ever - *The Dumping Ground*, Gareth Williams was tasked for a number of series with finding the 'real' Bradfield. He told me:

Bradfield became a combination of night-time aerial shots of Birmingham and ground locations in Newcastle. The biggest challenge was avoiding any glimpse of all the well-known Newcastle landmarks. When you are running a production on this scale proximity and practicality is all the rule. Most locations had to be thirty minutes or less from the centre of Newcastle. For Bradfield, Newcastle had the advantage of providing an incredible range of location and architecture within a very small radius, particularly compared to London. Also, rural locations like Morpeth and Hexham or a coastal cliff top scene you need aren't really that far away. For two years our production base was the Hadrian Yard in Wallsend, a former maintenance shed was turned into a stylised interior of the police station. Grim crime scenes and mortuary interiors were shot there as well. There were some very imaginative uses of locations - Queens Lane arches near the Bridge Hotel, mainly shot from the Keep nearby, became Bradfield's red light district. Tony Hill's home was in fact a former council office on Jesmond Road West, a building that had been converted in the 60s from a Regency terrace. One of the biggest challenges was the creation of Bradfield's Central Police Station - the original one was the site of the Bank of England's former Northern HQ. It had a *Goldfinger* feel to it, with a heavy vault door, boardroom, mullion windows, concrete mezzanine - it had been the second biggest bullion store in England! Semi-derelict, it was brought to life by production designers David Butterworth and John Collins. The second incarnation of the Police Station, production designed by Venita Gribble, was a former Rolls-Royce Switch Gear factory in

Team Valley. Steel cages, decking, gantries and even a testing module found a new life and identity for the series. Another interesting conversion was a wood-panelled banqueting refectory room in the 16th century Trinity House Hall which was used to create a Vaccaro/Caravaggio 'Old Masters' feel for a Series four episode *Hole in the Heart*. In all this we shouldn't forget the series' greatest asset- the acting prowess of Robson Green himself. One of the scripts proposed a scene where a woman throws herself in front of a train. Yes, this could be done, but it's the staging which would be too expensive and disruptive even for this scale of budget. Instead, because we knew we could use Robson Green's skilful acting reactions, we substituted a comparatively easier scenario where the woman appeared to fall over the Central Motorway footbridge. Because we utilised Robson's skills we were able to achieve the same dramatic impact with less expense and no angry passengers delayed at Newcastle Central!

The author vividly remembers visiting the set for *Wire in the Blood* where the Cruddas Park flats were being surrounded by a SWAT Team were besieging a sniper who was holding hostages. It was noted that the local population continued shopping totally unfazed by what they saw. All in a day's shopping.

Filming in Tynemouth.

55 Degrees North (2004)

Don Gilet as Nicky Cole
Dervla Kirwan as Claire Maxwell
Andrew Dunn as Sgt. Rick Astel
George Harris as Errol Hill
Mark Stobbart as PC Martin Clark
Jacqueline King as Georgina Hodge
Written by Timothy Prager

Undercover gumshoe Spender is scornful of Newcastle's designer makeover, but DS Nicky Cole in *55 Degrees North* is the opposite - he embraces it one hundred per cent.

55 Degrees North was the 2004-2006 swansong of Zenith North entertainment, who had given us *Byker Grove*. *55 Degrees North* was retitled *The Night Detective* in America and is a mould-breaking drama centring on a black 'night' detective on duty in the heart of the city of Newcastle. It claims to be the first lead Afro-Caribbean police role in BBC drama, setting the pace for *Luther* in more recent years.

Don Gilet plays Nicky Cole, who is permanently locked into manning the night shift. We meet him not as a noir hero, scuttling in the shadows, but as sharply dressed figure, driving his classic Mercedes Benz convertible over a busy Tyne Bridge with the panache of *Shaft* or *Starsky and Hutch*. This becomes the regular opening title, which sets the tone for the entire series. Cole is a stranger in a strange land. His family consists of nephew Matty and the sagacious 'elder' figure Uncle Errol. His work colleagues are an enigmatic mixture. Crown prosecutor Claire Maxwell, played by Dervla Kirwan, prompts the classic, 'Will they? Won't they get it together?' frisson, among the printers and stacks of case files and snobbish QCs. His boss won't release him from night shift (why? victimisation?) and there is at least one sinister colleague, played by Michael Hodgson. Cole, like Spender, has been relocated by his bosses in London - in his case for whistle-blowing activities on police corruption.

Episode one raises important questions and challenges the viewer. This is no by-the-numbers cop show, it has an undertow of ethnicity, community and multi-racial issues interplaying with the action. It questions North East attitudes to outsiders, too.

Episode one's pivotal sequence involves Cole's arrival in the city. He is pulled over in his Mercedes by the burly Sergeant Astel, who is unaware of who he really is. When asked why he's been stopped Cole replies, 'Driving whilst black?' and later quotes the Criminal Evidence Act of 1984. Astel, who has already called him 'a flash bastard', kicks in the Mercedes' rear light. Astel of course is more than surprised when he realises later that Cole is the new night detective. Cole, however, doesn't report Astel, 'Because I didn't want special treatment and you are a brother officer.' (Their relationship takes a very different form as the series progresses.)

There are constant personal hints of racism too. A banana is left on his desk, a local prostitute comments under interrogation that

she doesn't 'do blacks' as her boyfriend is in the BNP and there are plays on words, 'He's not a black man, he's a night detective'.

The other pivotal sequence is the audience's introduction to Newcastle. Cole chases an adversary at night through the heart of the City and Quayside. Geographically it doesn't quite follow a direct route - but who cares. A roller coaster camera takes us from the Bigg Market through Broad Chare, the concrete walkways of Dean Street and Cale Cross House, the High Level Bridge, culminating in a stunning sequence of a moving Swing Bridge glistening in the rain. In a later episode we see the Millennium Bridge and Sage Gateshead looking like a burnished extra-terrestrial craft. The Crown Prosecution Service apartment, of course, looks over the Millenium Bridge.

Episode one is the benchmark for the series. A re-branded Newcastle is a visually expressionist backdrop for Cole's nocturnal duties, which include a body pulled from the dark waters of the Tyne, a washed up Jane Doe. Then, courtesy of Sergeant Astel, there is the assumption that we have seen Cole walking into institutionalised racism - or have we? Creator, Tim Prager:

I had witnessed an incident involving a black policeman, a real night detective, in Cheltenham. This gave me the germ of an idea, and I researched further, meeting a black detective in Newcastle and the PR for Northumberland Police.

Newcastle was ideal for basing this drama. I had family connections, my mother's family were Armstrongs and for me it's a city that sings, a dazzling collision of architecture, a monument to time and endeavour in commercial and industrial history. Northumbria Police were modernising and establishing a new command structure. They were one of the first authorities to locate the CPS into the actual police station, hence the proximity and relationship between the characters played by Don Gilet and Dervla Kirwan. Near HMS *Calliope* - our police HQ - the Sage was being built. We decided for episode one to stage a foot chase using a Parisian Parkour (Street running) expert. Don did some of the stunts himself, but basically the night chase introduces the audience to the city of Newcastle.

Over the course of the series it is revealed that sergeant Astel is not a racist. His action of damaging Cole's headlight is prompted by his frustration over Cole's officious but correct quotation of the law, coupled with Astel being passed over for promotion. He is not racially motivated. It is in fact about Geordie attitudes to outsiders in general. I have always been fascinated by the neo-tribal loyalties in the region, even over a short distance between Geordies and Mackems in Sunderland.

In contrast to Cole's Newcastle nightlife world, where he patronises Quayside restaurants and is based at a police station. Cole's domestic life is located at Tynemouth. He, Matty and Errol occupy a clifftop cottage where family issues are played out - Matty's acceptance at school, the mystery of Matty's father's identity and the steadying lessons from uncle Errol who represents the first Afro-Caribbean generation to strive for emancipation in Britain. Errol brings examples to bear from his own cultural background, integrating with the local community with his boxing skills, replicating carnival and setting off a fire alarm with a jerk chicken barbecue.

The series is probably one of the first to address the multi-cultural aspects of Newcastle and North East life - Cole encounters, as part of his work load, Eastern Europeans, a Ugandan Asian, a Pakistani and a British-born kebab shop owner.

Nicky Cole's caseload is varied to say the least. The night detective must tackle robbery and vice and beyond. He is faced with a brothel trade war, an ecstasy dealer who is actually working under cover, dogging, abuse in care homes, the occasional murder and in the most innovative case, a Bigg Market slaying which uncovers a genetic cloning experiment. Other subjects include travellers, and a man refusing to sell in metric weight!

55 Degrees North was untimely in its end and as a TV drama it excelled in making the audience never take anything for granted:

Nicky Cole is initially a fish out of water in 55 Degrees North, an outsider coming in from the cold. Much of the drama comes from saying to him not that 'You're black' but 'You're not from here.' Outsiders and out-of-towners are coming into a changing place and I wanted to reflect this attitude shown towards them.

The series was edgier than a normal cop show and it showed a multi-cultural side to the North East that was rarely reflected then in TV or film. I tried to deal with unusual topics as when a Bigg Market death reveals a plot involving genetic engineering - not normally associated with party city! Equally important to me was Nicky's extended family in Tynemouth. I wanted to reverse the stereotype of black males abandoning their families and instead show a notion of brotherhood and care. Considering the BBC didn't originally want the series it ran to two series and eight million viewers!

Tim Prager

School for Seduction (2004)

Kelly Brook as Sophia Rosselini
Jake Canuso as Giovanni
Antonio Pellegrino as Italian Graduate (as Antonio Pelligrino)
Emma Lawson as Italian Graduate
Manuela Tundo as Italian Graduate
Neil Stuke as Craig
Jessica Johnson as Donna
Jody Baldwin as Gail
Tracy Hann as Laura
Dervla Kirwan as Clare
Emily Woof as Kelly
Nicola Blackwell as Lucy
Jane Holman as Kelly's Mum
Gez Casey as Kelly's Dad
Margi Clarke as Irene
Tim Healy as Derek
Directed by Sue Heel
Written by Sue Heel and Martin Heron

This movie sits uncomfortably between *Paper Marriage* and *The One and Only*, as a trilogy that attempts to reboot Newcastle as a backdrop for various forms of adult comedy. It was advertised as a meeting between *The Full Monty* and *Calendar Girls*, which turned out to be a false conceit.

An ostensibly Italian femme fatale arrives in Newcastle from Naples. Played by Kelly Brook, Sophia sets up an academy of seductive arts, presumably for the emancipation of North East women. Her pupils include a good repertory of actresses Margi Clarke, Dervla Kirwan and Emily Woof, who struggle portraying clichéd characters including the victim of a sexually manipulative boss, a husband who is more interested in his Fiat Spider and of course a resistant impotent husband played by Tim Healy. This is set pre-*Geordie Shore*, mainly it seems in the Copthorne Hotel and in and around a noisy Bigg Market. Most of the club interiors were shot inside studio two at Tyne Tees Television on City Road.

Top right: *Tim Healy and Margi Clarke.* Far Right: *Dervla Kirwan at Central Station.* Right: *Filming at Sandyford's Dinsdale Road.*

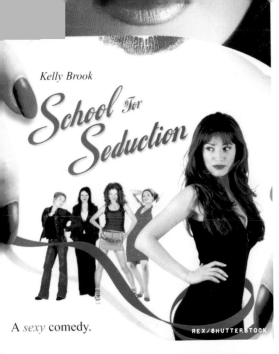

Kelly Brook

School for Seduction

A *sexy* comedy.

REX/SHUTTERSTOCK

NCJ MEDIA

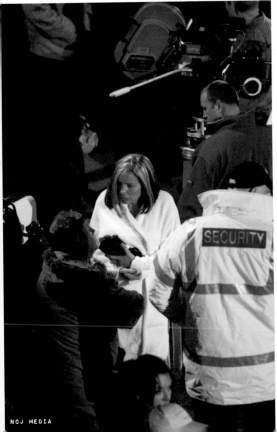

SECURITY

NCJ MEDIA

NCJ MEDIA

The film could be construed as patronising towards its female characters, almost in a *Viz* comic style. The resolution of each woman's 'lurv' problem recalls the clichés of a Whitehall farce. A naked man is stranded outside a house, the Fiat Spider is found in bed in crushed form and the 'pervy' boss is compromised in a photograph with a drag artist. There is even a lame attempt to clone *When Harry Met Sally's* diner orgasm scene by transferring it to Sabatini's Quayside restaurant. The sight of Sophia using her seduction techniques in a fish and chip shop are a wonder to behold. You've guessed it - the conclusion is she is NOT Italian.

Her pupils feel cheated - how do you think the audience felt? To say that this film went under the radar is an understatement.

Goal! (2005)

Kuno Becker as Santiago Munez
Anna Friel as Roz Harmison
Also starring Sean Pertwee, Alan Shearer, David Beckham and Brian Johnson
Written by Mike Jeffries and Adrian Butchart
Screenplay by Dick Clement and Ian La Frenais
Directed by Danny Cannon

Goal! was given the USA release title of *Goal! - The Dream Begins!* In the UK the film's subtitle was *'The Impossible Dream.'*

Both titles give a clear indication of the film's storyline. Kuno Becker plays Santiago Munez whose rags to riches odyssey on the football pitch leads him to eventual triumph at St James's Park. His journey begins with him crossing the Mexican border into the USA at the age of ten, clutching his football and a ragged picture of the FIFA world cup. One minute he is working as a teenager for his father's gardening business in California, the next, thanks to a football scout, he is trying out for the team on Tyneside. In some ways we are seeing Newcastle through the eyes of this hopeful young Mexican and the film aims to be the account of a young man's dream rather than the game of football.

A film like *Goal!* in the wrong hands could have ended up as a clichéd pastiche of *Roy of the Rovers* comic book exploits, but there was a dream production team on hand in the reserves to pull the film back from the brink. The dream team who turned the original story into a screenplay consisted of script maestros Dick Clement and Ian La Frenais. Suffice to say Tynesider Ian La Frenais' passion for his home team is demonstrated by the fact that in earlier years he substituted his own face onto a Newcastle team photograph on his bedroom wall. For him, St James's is a cathedral and this film is not a desecration:

The power of Goal! *is that it's simply the story of a talented boy and his football dream and we share his first visualisation and experiences of the North East where his sporting destiny lies - so far from his home and way of life. We see a foreigner's eye view of the North East. The director, Danny Cannon was a great shooter and he really captures this aspect in Santiago's training shots at Tynemouth. It says it all - all you need is a ball and friends to play with. I'm always amazed by the popularity of this so called macho film with female audiences -they really love it! there again it's an emotional film and it was made at the right time.*

Ian La Frenais

The duo succeeded in injecting the right amount of reality and twists that fate would throw in the path of such a young player, including health, moral problems and the dilemma of family loyalties, particularly to his doubting father.

The film's director was Danny Cannon who, in some ways, was the directorial equivalent of a method actor. He actually trained with a cast that skillfully combined actors with real football players. Cannon's direction and visualisation of Newcastle and the surrounding area is a tour-de-force. His aerial and ground shots of the city and the coast convey the wonder felt by young Santiago as he is given the chance to fulfil an impossible dream in Tyneside surroundings. The camera swoops down over the Tyne bridges, plunges into St James's Park and races to the sound of Oasis as Munez trains on the Long Sands at Tynemouth - the latter location made by default when weather and road works terminated central Newcastle filming.

Thanks to Danny Cannon we share Santiago Munez's vision on and off the pitch and the director was clearly impressed by what he saw here.

By all accounts the filming was an ordeal, the forty-two day schedule was hampered by snow and the cast often felt they were perpetually drowning in ice-cold water. Football matches were filmed with the co-operation of FIFA and Cannon effortlessly integrated real matches with staged ones. You can't see the joins.

It is also claimed that actress Anna Friel, once she had landed her role, spoke in a Geordie accent twenty-four hours a day until the film was complete.

Along with the thespians there are on and off pitch appearances by David Beckham, Sven Goran Eriksson, Alan Shearer and many other football stars. It is a mark of the film's realism that they don't look embarrassed or uncomfortable in their roles. Neither does AC/DC frontman Brian Johnson, who is seen watching and commenting on the climactic match in an LA bar.

Most of the film was shot in Newcastle though some apartment interiors were shot in Kings Cross.

The film's soundtrack is exceptional, it includes three previously unavailable Oasis songs, Noel Gallagher's *Who Put the Weight of the World on My Shoulders?* and a remix of *Morning Glory*.

We follow Santiago from going on as a substitute when Newcastle play Fulham, to taking a free kick when they are confronted by Liverpool - it says something for the skill of Danny Cannon and the editor that you cannot see where the extra goals were added in post-production.

Anna Friel and Kuno Becker cross the Gateshead Millenium Bridge.

The Tournament (2009)

Robert Carlyle as Father MacAvoy
Kelly Hu as Lai Lai Zhen
Ian Somerhalder as Miles Slade
Liam Cunningham as Powers
Ving Rhames as Joshua Harlow
Directed by Scott Mann

A twelve-million dollar production starring Robert Carlyle and Ving Rhames, this is the story of the ultimate in high stakes. The world's leading hit-men must eliminate each other in a secret competition where the last man standing receives ten million pounds. The whole bloody competition is watched on CCTV by millionaire gamblers. The competition takes place every seven years in an unsuspecting British city. Yes, you've guessed it, this year the tournament seems to take place in Middlesbrough with a measure of Gateshead thrown in. A reputedly troubled production, *The Tournament* is no *Running Man*, or *Rollerball*, as Carlyle and Rhames struggle with the clichés. The dereliction of Gateshead old High Street is glimpsed behind Carlyle and in a bizarre climax in Middlesborough he highjacks the No.192 double-decker bus bound for 'Easingwold'. Does this mean that in the next *Mad Max* opus we will see Tom Hardy high-jacking the Fab 56 bus to Newcastle?

For some reason, and it's not for lack of talent on screen, *The Tournament* just doesn't deliver.

Right: *A pale substitute for Gateshead High Street.*

ROBERT CARLYLE   KELLY HU   AND VING RHAMES

THE TOURNAMENT

DEATH BY ELIMINATION

Tracy Beaker Returns (2010-12)
The Dumping Ground (2013-)
Wolfblood (2010-)

NCJ MEDIA

After the demise of *Byker Grove* (and the liquidation of its production company Zenith Entertainment) the core production team, now based in Morpeth, have continued, mainly for CBBC, to produce prestigious and award-winning children's drama. Two of the series *Tracy Beaker Returns* and *The Dumping Ground*, based on the character created by Jacqueline Wilson, have involved the very skilful fictionalisation of locations, particularly the care homes, in and around Newcastle - although it is never named geographically. As with *Byker Grove*, *Tracy Beaker Returns* and series one of *The Dumping Ground* found themselves in the shadow of a building landmark that had seen many uses. The interiors were shot in the grand gothic villa building originally known as Jesmond Towers, which changed from a family residence to a convent and convent school in the early 1900s known as La Sagesse. Suitable only for interior shots (due to La Sagesse's grand exterior) the TV exterior of the fictitious care home Elm Tree House was in fact the exterior of the adjoining priest's or father's house, which may have been a farmhouse. Series two of *The Dumping Ground* sees a new care home known as Ash Dene Ridge which is in fact a private property at Rowlands Gill. Following the demolition of La Sagesse, interiors are now shot at Charles Thorp Comprehensive School on Hookergate Campus, again at Rowlands Gill. The production has also featured Kingston Park, Chillingham Road and the City Hall. It remains the most successful CBBC production ever.

The Rowlands Gill locations now double (since 2012) for the award winning Debbie Moon created series *Wolfblood* - following the trials and tribulations of teenagers who are part 'lycanthrope'. Unusually, *Wolfblood* does actually identify Newcastle and the surrounding area landmarks, much to the relief of location manager Gareth Williams who has spent much of his career on productions avoiding any local identity.

Hum, Tum Aur Ghost
(Me, You And The Ghost) (2010)

Directed by Kabeer Kaushik
Co-written, produced and starring Arshad Warsi.
Also starring Dia Mirza.

The Bollywood industry is increasingly focusing on Newcastle as a
potential filming location. Fortune struck twice in 2010. The movie
Kaun Bola saw the staging on Grey Street of a spectacular car
stunt co-ordinated by Rocky Taylor. Shoppers and passers-by were
treated to the spectacle of a red Volkswagen Beetle flying past the
Theatre Royal in mid-air.

In the same year the city played host to *Hum, Tum Aur Ghost*
created by Arshad Warsi and starring the former Miss India, Dia
Mirza, as Gehna. The movie is a mixture, as you would expect, of
fantasy and romance - in some ways a musical version of
Ghostbusters, with a dash of *The Sixth Sense* and *Topper* thrown
in.

Warsi plays Armaan, a highly successful photographer who
discovers that he - and only he - can see and communicate with a
group of souls crossing between life and death. As the plot unfolds
with both elements of comedy and tragedy he helps the stranded
souls to find peace and complete their journey out of purgatory.
Needless to say his gift causes total misunderstanding with those
around him, particularly his partner Gehna.

Though not very successful, the film demonstrates how the city
of Newcastle effortlessly merges into the world of Bollywood
spectacle - Grey Street is bathed in light for a romantic ballet, the
High Level Bridge is suffused in blue light, a fashion shoot
spectacle materialises at Grey's Monument and a ghostly boy
literally walks straight through the traffic outside City Hall. The
Castle Keep and the Long Stairs aren't left out either and the most
stunning sequence takes place on a fogbound Tyne Bridge when
Armaan meets the spokesman for the ghosts who is a mentor from
the other side.

Arshad Warsi was extremely complimentary about the co-
operation of Newcastle City Council. I hope their co-operation was
not in vain as he said a number of people thought the film was shot
in Budapest! More Bollywood films are planned for the region.

Dead Frequency (2010)

Stephen Mason as Sam Stuart
Cheryl Moody as Jenny
Michaela Marshall as Emily Jasper
Faye Ormston as Diane
Simon Hodgson as Kevin
Written and Directed by Rob Burrows

Sam, a late night radio talk show host, seems to have it all in terms of his job and his love for Emily. He also has problems involving depression and alcohol dependency. The least of his problems is that he is a vampire and one who is able to go out during the day. *Dead Frequency* uses locations that include the Castle Keep, Central Station, Newcastle Civic Centre bell tower, Star FM in Sunderland, Birtley Hall, Sage Gateshead, the Baltic Centre and Saltwell Park.

Despite its clear budgetary limitations the film has some chillingly effective moments. Essentially a black comedy, it was written and directed by Rob Burrows, an academic writer and emergency nurse practitioner when he is not behind the camera. Burrows founded Solarus Films in the North East in 2010, when his original script for *Dead Frequency* was procrastinated over by the BBC.

Undeterred by this, Burrows decided to make and finance the film himself over a period of six months.

He has used Solarus to produce, direct, write and co-write further films - these include *Entwinement*, a psycho-drama set against the background of Newcastle night life, mainly filmed at the legendary Tup Tup Palace nightclub, and *Flowerman* which deals with the theme of the abduction of a mother and wife by what is described as a 'forensically-aware psychopath'. These and his other films are not straightforward genre pieces, they all contain dark often comedic twists. The two films mentioned both garnered fifteen international film festival nominations between them, *Flowerman* achieving two winning awards.

Burrows is one of a new breed of independent film maker, self-financing and using a distributor to exploit the platform of digital market outlets. Though his films have achieved guest screenings in local cinemas, their real exposure throughout the world has come through Amazon Prime, Google Play, Vimeo and Tubi TV.

Audiences from USA to Japan lap them up.

In the film making world of today fortune favours the brave as never before. Solarus now looks set to transcend its local roots by attracting world stars to promote its future offerings. It looks likely at the time of writing that Hollywood actor Patrick Bergen will star in their forthcoming zom-rom *Train Set*!

Unconditional (2011)

Christian Cooke as Liam
Harry Mcentire as Owen
Madeleine Clarke as Kristen
Melanie Hill as Maureen
James Bolam as the Landlord
Directed by Bryn Higgins

Bryn Higgins' *Unconditional* has elements of psycho-drama and black comedy.

Maureen, a disabled mother, lives with her twin children, Owen and Kristen (once again, her flat is located on the ubiquitous Cruddas Park Estate). Their financial woes could be relieved when they are visited by the super cool financial adviser/loan shark,

Roker Pier, Sunderland. © Stone City Films Ltd

Liam. Liam's effect on the twins is instantaneous. Kristen is obsessed with him and sees him as boyfriend material and Owen, who he befriends, sees him as a portal to a lifestyle he has only ever read or dreamt about.

To confuse the issue, Liam seems only interested in Owen. Liam and Owen embark on a night out in Newcastle, which Owen finds intoxicating in more ways than one. Ostensibly as a joke, when they are carousing in Liam's designer apartment, which of course overlooks the Quayside and the Millennium Bridge, Liam presents him with women's clothes. In what seems a night on the 'Toon' joke, Owen is persuaded to pose as a woman and hit the city high spots. In a visually arresting sequence of Central Newcastle nightlife, the duo's slightly sinister journey by car into clubland takes on an extraordinarily glossy lustre. Liam is clearly fulfilling a fantasy, rather than playing a prank and Owen is clearly flattered,

confused and possibly enjoying the attention of male onlookers. For Owen and for the audience, this city homage sequence, which boasts dazzlingly evocative camera and lighting effects, has a dreamlike quality.

Liam becomes more controlling and in a Cinderella-like moment insists that Owen takes Kristen's identity and name.

As the plot unfolds, Liam becomes unpredictable, angry and disturbing in his manipulation. Kristen discovers the relationship between the loan shark and her brother, which has a traumatic effect. Liam's final possessive act bizarrely is to book/imprison them both in the honeymoon suite of a garish seaside B&B owned by former 'Likely Lad' James Bolam. It was Bolam's first north east shoot for twenty-five years.

Director Bryn Higgins' visual style isn't just restricted to the city, equally stunning are his location shots of the north east coast from South Shields to Roker and Redcar. In an unforgettable scene, Owen is forced to strip off his female clothes and possibly Kristen's identity, as the waves crash in on him and he is abandoned - exposed and naked to the world and its elements. This is a rites of passage film with a dark twist. There was a real-life dramatic twist when the encroaching waves actually destroyed a camera when filming another scene on Roker Pier, according to director Bryn Higgins:

The film is a mixture of psychodrama and romance and is difficult to market as a conventional comedy. It was originally set in the Midlands, but we settled on the North East because of the incredible range of scenery and architecture which are available to you over a small distance in and around Newcastle. It also helped that our Director of Photography, Paul Otter comes from the area. For a film of this scale, London can be very difficult in time consuming trips between locations. Melanie Hill was very good as the twins' mother and of course she is very rooted in the place. James Bolam loved the script and proved again that he is a highly perceptive actor.

Cinematically, filming in September I was able to make use of the long evening light. It really brought out the urban landscape and the bridges and scale around Liam's flat on the Quayside. We got great shots for very little money though we had to work quickly both in the city and on the coast. My favourite scenes apart from Tynemouth and Saltburn, are where Liam and Owen drive into the city at night, which I portrayed as a sort of Wonderland.

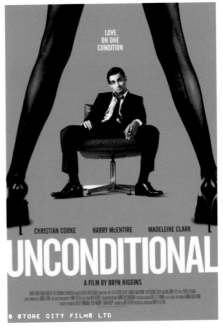

Top: *Christian Cooke with Newcastle and Gateshead's Bridgescape.* Above left: *Madeleine Clarke with those flats!*

Unconditional had a certain amount of freewheeling and improvisation to it which contributes to Liam's volatile behaviour. Liam does love Owen but he is a dark angel - wounded and damaged in his obsession. If there is any message it's is that the path of true love is not easy - be true to yourself and don't be pushed. I'm pleased to say that the film has taken on a life particularly in festivals and is reflective of the whole transgender climate which is coming into the mainstream.

Bryn Higgins, Director

Unconditional was made before transgender issues became prominent in popular entertainment. Movies like *The Danish Girl* and particularly the BBC transgender comedy drama series *Boy Meets Girl*, co-written by Cramlington's Elliott Kerrigan and filmed in Newcastle, have both raised the question that you should be judged for who you are, not what you are. *Unconditional* deals with control in a relationship and a person's ability to overcome that and is a milestone that understandably is now gaining a lot of retrospective interest and admiration.

Unconditional *gave me a challenging role
and a very good team to work with. On
such a small budget it is incredible what
they achieved in terms of the colours and
images particularly of Newcastle at night.*

Melanie Hill

Geordie Shore (2011-)

Watching television used to afford audiences an escape from reality. Today audiences escape *into* reality. Reality television is here to stay as it grants everyone the Andy Warhol promise of fame for fifteen minutes. Reality stars often get years of fame which can bring wealth, notoriety or tragedy. Some view it as trash, others see it as the twenty-first century equivalent of Hogarth.

MTV brought *Geordie Shore* to our screens five years ago and it shows no sign of disappearing. It is the media equivalent of Marmite, there is no middle ground in its criticism. The producers describe it as 'a group of lads and lasses from Newcastle living and working together'. With names like Gaz, Sophie, Charlotte-Letitia, Holly, Vicky and any other name that comes through the revolving door of fame, we witness literally and metaphorically their mental, romantic, and physical ups and downs. This brash combination of drunken antics, rows and sex on night vision cameras was originally played out in their accommodation on Carlton Terrace in Jesmond, then relocated to the Oceana Business Park in Wallsend. Outside the 'frat house' the action hits Newcastle night clubs and has extended around the world to clubbing locations in Ibiza, Magaluf, Mexico, Australia and beyond.

Geordie Shore is a contradiction, it has prompted questions in the House of Commons about its neo-pornographic nature and promotion of alcohol, yet by the same token it has had a proven effect on increasing tourism to the partying aspects of Newcastle City centre. Chris Hooton, entertainment writer for *The Metro* wrote: 'To be shocked by the lasciviousness of *Geordie Shore* is like being shocked by the lack of nutrition in a Pot Noodle.' Journalist Miriam Phipps-Bertram comments:

As both a viewer and a young person from the North East, I enjoy watching *Geordie Shore*. I'm not offended by it or see it as a threat to Newcastle's tourism or nightlife – in fact, I'm pretty sure it has encouraged people from all over the country to come and visit the city. It's good fun and in the end, that's all the programme is about; a few young people living and working together and having a laugh. There is no malice in this reality soap, it is there to entertain.

The programme is witty and realistic and also looks into other aspects of young people's lives, such as friendships and romantic relationships. The personalities on *Geordie Shore* are relatable and lovable – they even refer to themselves as one big 'family'. As time has gone on, they have become stylists and business people; bringing out their own lines of make-up and clothes. Essentially, they have become people that the public look up to and idolise.

Geordie Shore shows Newcastle as 'the city' to get very drunk in and have a fantastic night with friends. I think it's fair to say that that, although it does not give the impression that Newcastle is a cosmopolitan and civilised night out, it's not that type of amusement most young people are looking for. If you came to Newcastle, much like on a standard *Geordie Shore* episode, you would see people falling about in the streets, drunk in the gutter in tight skirts and high heels, however, name me a city where this doesn't happen? The drinks are cheap and the people are 'up for a laugh', giving people a great night out. That is not to say that you can't find a sophisticated night out in Newcastle. If you know where to go, you'll find it, and this side can be seen in *Geordie*

Shore when the housemates go on 'dates' or for one to one drinks, away from the big group.

Bars such as Florita's, Madame Koo's and the Riverside night club have all become iconic places to go – to the point where I have been asked on several nights out in Newcastle where to find them.

It's also not just about the night out. Quintessential shots of the city are included in the opening credits as well as in the background of the famous 'face to camera' interviews – where the housemates give their real opinions on the past events.

I think *Geordie Shore*, although partially scripted, is an accurate representation of how many young people live their lives all over the country and behind closed doors. Work hard, party harder. I would even go so far as to say that it is probably not as shocking as it could be!

Miriam Phipps-Bertram

Tyneside actor Victoria Elliot commented on the negative effects:

I have to say I have watched the first three series and then I just couldn't watch any more, it became a parody of itself if that's possible. I think it's a damning indictment of the times isn't it? I really feel sorry for those kids, they are put in a house and put in a position where they might make terrible decisions which are filmed and then viewed across the globe. I worry about the psychological damage that it will do to them.

Victoria Elliot

In a perverse way *Geordie Shore* succeeded where contemporary drama serials like *Quayside* failed. Like it or not it is the nearest we will ever get to a true soap opera. Cast members Gaz and Holly have both released singles - they both failed to chart, unlike *Byker Grove's* PJ and Duncan!

Right: Brenda Blethyn and the Vera *crew filming on the High Level Bridge.*

Vera (2011-)

Brenda Blethyn as DCI Vera Stanhope (28 episodes, 2011-2017)
Jon Morrisonas DC Kenny Lockhart (23 episodes, 2011-2016)
David Leonas DS Joe Ashworth (16 episodes, 2011-2014)
Riley Jonesas DC Mark Edwards (14 episodes, 2011-2016)
Paul Ritteras Billy Cartwright (12 episodes, 2011-2013)

If *Wire in the Blood* masks the real identity of its locations *Vera* makes no secret of them DCI Vera Stanhope, the creation of Ann Cleeves, works under the jurisdiction of the fictitious 'Northumberland City and Police Authority'. Brenda Blethyn's portrayal of Vera shows her as a dishevelled, obsessive investigator of crime. She battles her own inner demons and is surrounded by the bitter sweet memories of her father in a gloomy cottage on Holy Island.

Andrew Bainbridge, the former location manager for the production, told me that the original pilot episode was angled to a more comfortable rural setting. He said:

Vera was originally seen living in a setting like Phoenix House in Central Newcastle. Then she was deliberately isolated into her late father's cottage, which gives a completely different feel. Visually and location wise, we went for a feel that combined North East grit and beauty, it had to be tough as well as lovely. When you watch *Vera* and locations like Blyth and Druridge Bay there is no denying their visual impact, but you can see that man, his industries and search for energy has had an impact on the landscape as well.

It's a very important combination behind the drama. We never wanted it to be too idyllic, in fact we call all these locations 'Veraland!' In series one and two, Vera was rarely seen in Newcastle but in three and four the city really comes into play and opens up. The main police station was located at Swan Hunter ship yard, then after series five it relocated to the Oceana Business Park in Wallsend. Sometimes one set will be a combination of very different buildings. A military barracks was in fact a cut-together of TT Electronics in Bedlington, St Mary's College and Prudhoe Hospital. Of course the Quayside, the bridges, the Baltic and the Sage all bring their impact to the story as well. Without a doubt my favourite location was the wonderful sweep of the concrete pedestrian walkway by Manors car park. It gave me great satisfaction to see a stunt man at last being thrown off it - onto a mat of course. Our other favourite spots on the 'Veraland' tour are Whitley Bay, Tynemouth Pier and of course Vera's favourite soul-searching place, the wonderful Rendezvous Cafe at Whitley Bay.

Andrew Bainbridge, Location Manager

Right: The Vera *film crew geting ready to fish a 'body' from the Tyne. In the background those flats again, after their 2010 revamp.*

Harrigan (2013)

Ian Whyte as Ronnie
Stephen Tompkinson as Harrigan
Craig Conway as Dunstan
Gillian Kearney as Bridie Wheland
Maurice Roëves as Billy Davidson
Directed by Vince Woods

Middlesbrough and Newcastle supply backgrounds for a
potentially hard-edged production directed by Vince Woods.
Detective Harrigan stars Stephen Tomkinson as a DI returning to
the North East from Hong Kong to investigate the death of his
daughter at the hands of Triads in Newcastle. Much of the action
is centred in a fictitious sink-estate named Monkshire where
Harrigan reopens a boarded up police section station. Partly based
on real events during the British winter of discontent (1978-79),
the section station is besieged by a local mob and Harrigan must
face down his daughter's killer. There's a particularly vicious
portrayal of a clown-faced psychopath played brilliantly by local
actor Craig Conway, previously seen as a hit-man in *The
Tournament*. Tomkinson as usual, masters the role of concealing
inner personal turmoil behind actually focusing on the job in hand.
Detective Harrigan is an example of great potential being crippled
by low production values. The production company Tall Tree Films
also produced the Newcastle detective drama *The Bait Room*.

HARRIGAN

WRITTEN BY MULTI-DECORATED COP **ARTHUR MCKENZIE**

I, Daniel Blake (2016)

Dave Johns as Daniel
Hayley Squires as Katie
Sharon Percy as Sheila
Briana Shann as Daisy
Dylan McKiernan as Dylan
Directed by Ken Loach

Newcastle has set a bench mark in confrontational cinema. Amber Films Workshop Collective has constantly committed the marginal communities of the region to film and still photography since 1969. More recently the Iranian/British director Tina Gharavi stunned international audiences with *I Am Nasrine*, the story of a brother and sister transposed from their native Tehran to start a new life in housing projects in Newcastle - a film that doesn't compromise in its portrayal of the positives and negatives facing political immigrants. Gharavi's work has been quoted as sharing the spirit of Ken Loach. The film making prowess of eighty-year old Ken Loach, Britain's most confrontational film maker, shows no signs of diminishing.

    I, Daniel Blake focuses on the lives of two individuals trapped in the labyrinth of the benefit system. Daniel is a widower signed off work due to a heart attack. He fails a 'fit for work' benefits test and is told to go on JobSeeker's Allowance which requires him to seek work. At the job centre he meets Katie, a single mother forced by unsocial housing conditions out of London. The film follows their spiralling fortunes, sometimes humorous - but mostly unflinchingly bleak. The location is present day Newcastle and the small production team filmed in the City Library, Byker, Northumberland Street, Shieldfield and Jarrow. Ken Loach told me about his decision to film in the North East:

In Newcastle we worked on a very tight schedule, we only had five weeks so we had to shoot fast but I like that because tight schedules give you a positive energy to work with. Newcastle's architecture is terrific, though there are some recent examples of phoney overblown buildings which need to be demolished. I didn't really have as much time as I wanted to explore.

    The film could apply to any town. In the film there is a single mother driven out of London by high rents. I found an incredible

contrast where poverty very clearly exists in a city that seems to be thriving. I felt this when I was filming at the Monument, people struggling with the trap of benefits sat near people with big shopping bags. I felt the sense of a city where poverty exists alongside prosperity. Newcastle has a rich culture and the area has a strong sense of resistance, an irrepressible humour and a rich and imaginative language.

Ken Loach

Daniel Blake is played by Dave Johns. Johns has carved out a successful career as a stand-up comedian for over two decades. He had played small parts in *George Gently* and Cookson dramas and he performed annually with other established comedians in classic plays staged at the Edinburgh Festival. These included *Twelve Angry Men* and *The Odd Couple*, it was this experience which led him to audition for Ken Loach's Newcastle based film.

Dave told me:

It was a real challenge to go from one day on a set in a small part - to playing one of two central parts spread over nine weeks of filming. Ken Loach is a very passionate man as a director and he also has a very humorous side. I was playing opposite Hayley Squires as Katie and it was ironic that she and I had the most chemistry between us when we were auditioning without being told we'd got the parts. Ken had obviously weighed up what he'd seen happening between us. I couldn't believe I was filming on the streets of Byker where I had grown up. When you are acting the main part, like Daniel Blake, you are literally up there without a net. The performances really exposed us because there is no music in the film to underline anything. Before a scene, Ken would say to us, 'Listen to each other, find the truth and the emotion in yourselves, react truthfully in front of the camera, be truthful in the moment.'

It is not true that much of this film is improvised, we worked to an incredible script by Paul Laverty. The mark of great writing is that it disappears when you make the words your own.

The impact of the film? I've attended six festival screenings all over Europe and the reaction is always the same, indignant audiences often in tears. In Switzerland, where there were eight thousand people in attendance, you could hear a pin drop. Ken's skill is that he works very unobtrusively, he gives a voice to people who have no voice. It asks you to judge whether Daniel and Katie

are 'strivers or skivers'. As for the image of Newcastle, well there will be those who say here comes the 'Ken Loach train of misery'. For me Newcastle has always been a friendly and welcoming place. This is a story of real life and the truth can be bleak. I've never met a comedian yet who doesn't tell me they are looking forward to performing in this city.

Dave Johns, Actor.

Ken Loach has won his second Palme D'Or, for this portrayal of a system summarised by Daniel as a 'monumental farce'. Critic Pamela Hutchinson describes it as 'a desperately important exposé of an unfair system'.

Through the past, darkly.

Producers, and particularly their location managers, find that Newcastle has a bewildering range of architectural styles. Over the years the burgeoning industry of costume films and dramas has taken full advantage of this. In 1969, Ken Russell filmed key scenes for *Women in Love* in Northumberland, Newcastle and Gateshead. When Gudrun, played by Glenda Jackson, is seen wandering less than salubrious backstreets, she is in fact wandering in Half Moon Street outside the present Central Bar in Gateshead (just around the corner from Bottle Bank, used in the 1961 movie *Payroll*). The Half Moon Hotel which was involved in the wandering scene, is now demolished.

Historic locations really came into their own when Catherine Cookson's multi-million selling novels of North East life were adapted for television. Eighteen of her books were televised between 1989 and 2001, beginning with *The Fifteen Streets* and ending with *A Dinner Of Herbs*. Produced by Ray Marshall, these adaptations were as successful worldwide as their print counterparts. Sean Bean, Catherine Zeta-Jones and Robson Green were just some of the rising stars featured. The Quayside's cobbled Hanover Street became a 1850s crowded thoroughfare in *The Glass Coffin*, a Gateshead factory even became a mine. Remember - Cookson had been a meticulous researcher going down a mine herself, so everything had to be right. Other memories of Cookson productions come from location manager Christine Lewellyn-Reeve:

In the summer of 1993 I was the Location Manager for Catherine Cookson's, *The Dwelling Place*. A co-production between Tyne Tees Television and Festival Films, it was set in 1830 and featured not only remote countryside but also the Newcastle City Centre of the time.

An outstanding memory is that of me organising the filming on one of the Tall Ships due to arrive for the Tall Ships' Race second visit to Newcastle in 1993. One of the main characters, in disgrace, goes to sea and then returns some time later. The script, ideally required a shot of this action, of him boarding the ship and then after a costume and make-up change, disembarking the ship a year or so later.

Top: *Waiting for the* Eye of the Wind. Left: *Hanover Street dressed for the 1850s.*

CHRISTINE LLEWELLYN-REEVE

CHRISTINE LLEWELLYN-REEVE

Not an easy ask. However, luck was with us in that we had some ships of the correct period during our filming schedule of eight weeks docking in the city centre. I did some research, and contacted the organising authorities. The ship had to be as authentic as possible (we would dress it and the quayside on its arrival). The *Eye of The Wind*, a UK training ship seemed to be the first choice for its age and looks and also because it was due to arrive at exactly the right day required. Weather and tides have to be taken into account, and in discussion via radio with the ship's captain, travelling towards us in the North Sea, I got the reply that they were certainly up for it, but I would have to regularly liaise with him so they could fulfil the arrival times of the event and our filming in what would be a very narrow window of opportunity.

I had to find a quayside outside of the city centre (because too many modern buildings would be visible, it would be difficult to frame out of shot, and where we might get in the way of the national event). The Quay at Shepherd's Offshore was a possibility, and they were fantastic in allowing us to arrange for the *Eye of the Wind* to dock briefly on their quay on its way into Newcastle. The depth of the water at different tide times all had to be taken into consideration. I shall never forget the image of the beautiful tall ship, appearing out of the misty morning like a Turner painting, as it made its way up river towards us, while we, a second unit, were all poised with the props for the ship, the actors dressed and ready and the quayside set with all the trappings of a busy port of the 1830s.

I was in constant contact with the captain who navigated his path up the Tyne with perfect timing. We had four hours within the tides to film so that the ship could continue safely on its journey up the Tyne and arrive as scheduled. Another magic moment and I still have the honorary ships *Eye of the Wind* crew hat to prove it.

The Glass Virgin, another Tyne Tees Television and Festival films joint production, was set in Newcastle in the mid-nineteenth century. The story was centred around the glass manufacturing industry in Newburn which was still operational when we filmed this novel.

One of the scenes involved the wealthy family driving through the slums of Victorian Newcastle at night in an open carriage. Forth Banks at the time of filming was still cobbled with the multi-storey old warehouses bordering the steep cobbled road on the river side and nothing on the other side but steep rough banks held in place with high brick supports. It was pretty much an unchanged period view. It was about the only location we actually had to apply for, and enforce a total road closure for two or three days to enable the filming, but also where our Art Department could transform the semi-derelict warehouses and bring them back to life as tenement dwellings of the 1850s. I risked life and limb recceing the interiors with the landlords and establishing safety parameters for access and where we could place interior lights for the shoot. The Art Department using scaffolding rigs and cherry pickers reframed windows, built temporary balconies and dressed many windows and high doors to create the illusion. I had to resort to the ancient Greek method of finding ways through a labyrinth of staircases and rooms with the help of the landlords marking out safe passages through the building with hazard tape so that extras and crew could get access to the windows for filming.

Everything had been 'dressed' and set to favour the left hand warehouse side for the Director's original requested camera angle of looking downhill. It even meant that the Art Department had also had to utilise tricks to disguise the bottom of the Metro Bridge in the distance with 'dingle' and other dressing in an arch that framed the shot without actually being on the bridge itself. This all took days of work and weeks of preparation. The entire street was 'dressed', and on the night, the lamps were fired up, extras were placed in windows via ladders and cherry pickers, children were playing in the streets, chickens and dogs with their wranglers were on hand, braziers were lit to create smoke and atmosphere and the carriage and horses were moved from their safe haven in the Dove's Car Park at the top of Forth Banks and was waiting, poised for its downhill race.

The Director arriving for the first time on set and checking the shot was silent for a few moments and then said 'I think the shot would be better if we reversed and looked the other way up the hill' Need I say what the reaction was!

I seem to remember the Producer and Designer managed to find a diplomatic and artistic way of convincing him it might not be such a good option! All we had to do from then on was make sure the horses could actually get back up the hill on the wet cobbles for the numerous takes. No one realised it could be a problem and each time the carriage had to be unhitched and manhandled up the hill. It is amazing what you learn in filming!

Christine Llewellyn-Reeve

The Constant Location

Even as I write, this book is going out of date. Newcastle continues to be a location of choice for TV and Film producers and directors. *Vera* is currently filming in the Lit and Phil on West Road, Davina McCall was filming in Leazes Park recently for a new TV Game show – *The Line*. A film about Keith Crombie, *The Geordie Jazz Man*, the long-time owner of the Jazz Café on Pink Lane was recently premiered at the Long Beach Indie International Film Festival in California. ITV are screening *Car Wars*, which follows traffic officers from Northumbria Police around the 'Toon' - the director makes constant use of the features of the City that have attracted film makers since *On the Night of the Fire* - the bridges and 'levels' of the City flash in quick cuts between the car chases.

Thousands flocked to Newcastle City Centre on a sunny September Sunday morning to see the stars, both human and mechanical of the forthcoming *Transformers: The Last Knight*. The familiar yellow 'Bumblebee' car - a £1.7m Lamborghini, roared with other super-cars up Grey Street, around Monument and onto Grainger Street which had been closed to public access to allow filming. As the cars sped past the entrance to the Grainger Market, rubble fell from a skip which had been hoisted above the street to mimic falling masonary. One of the stars, Josh Duhamel, said 'It's one of the most beautiful cities I've ever seen.'

In a small volume it would be impossible to achieve an encyclopaedic catalogue of every film and TV programme made in Newcastle. However, I hope I have brought attention to shows and films you may not have been aware of and will go out and seek online or on DVD.

Even as an avid fan of film, TV and Newcastle, I was amazed to see that the Internet Movie Database lists over two-hundred films and TV programmes have been made in Newcastle upon Tyne. Some of these are listed below, and range from Geordie stars playing their home town (Pet Shop Boys, Roy 'Chubby' Brown, Alan Shearer) to the mundane (*Changing Rooms* & *Location, Location, Location*) to the bizarre (*Dogging: A Love Story, The Bad Samaritan Must Die!, Tyne & Wear Metro: The Musical* and *Zombie Women of Satan 2*)!

140 (2009)
20,000 Employees Entering Lord Armstrong's Elswick Works, Newcastle-upon-Tyne (1900)
55 Degrees North (2004–2005)
6 to Midnight (1974)
A Dinner of Herbs (2000 TV Series)
A Knight in Camelot (1998 TV Movie)
A Tribute to Jackie Milburn: The Jackie Milburn Story(1989 Video)
Airline (1998–)
All Over the Place (2011–)
Almost Married (2014)
Alternative Therapy (1998)
And a Nightingale Sang (1989 TV Movie)
Anything Legal Considered (1968–)
April's Fools (2015)
Auf Wiedersehen, Pet (1983–2004)
Back with the Boys Again - Auf Wiedersehen Pet 30th Anniversary Reunion (2013 Video)
Beaten (2005 TV Movie)
Beggars' Teeth (2012)
Behind the Scenes of Total Hell (2013)
Bewick's Mambo (2008)
Billy Connolly: Live (2002 Video)
Billy Elliot (2000)
Birthday Girl (III) (2016)
Blind Ambition (2000 TV Movie)
Bob Dylan: Dont Look Back (1967)
Breeze Block (2002–)
British Gangsters: Faces of the Underworld (2012–)
Byker Grove (1989–2006)
Byker (1983)

Bystander (1998)
Chain Letters (1987–1997)
Chances (III) (2014)
Changing Rooms (1997–2004)
Close & True (2000–)
Clown Syndrome (2014 TV Movie)
Come Again (1998)
Come Back (2008)
Cutting Edge (1990–)
Day of the People (2016)
Daylight Robbery (2008)
Dense Fear Bloodline (2012)
Director's Cut (II) (2006)
Dispatches (1987–)
Dispatches (1987–)
Dogging: A Love Story (2009)
Driven (1994 TV Short)
Drunken Butterflies (2014)
Dystopolis (2011)
Electricity (2014)
England on Film (2003–)
Eyeless (2008)
Final Call (2010)
Finney (1994–)
Fire & Brimstone (TV Movie)
Firm Friends (TV Mini-Series 1992)
Football Diaries (2004 TV Series)
Frank (I) (2008)
Frank (II) (2012)
Gabriel & Me (2001)
Geordie Shore (2011–)
Get Carter (1971)
Goal II: Living the Dream (2007)
Goal! The Dream Begins (2005)
Got to Run (2011)
Harrigan (2013)
Helen (I) (2008)
Henry (III) (2012)
Holding On (II) (2015)
Hum Tum Aur Ghost (2010)

Hunted: The Pick Up (2011 Video)
I, Daniel Blake (2016)
In a Metal Mood (1996)
In Our Name (2010)
In Which We Serve (1942)
Inbetween (1999)
Inspector George Gently (2007–)
Jealousy (I) (2015)
Joe Maddison's War (2010 TV Movie)
Just Another Day (2001 TV Movie)
Keegan on Keegan (1992 Video)
Killing Time (1998)
King's Ransom (2000)
Knox (2015)
Latch (2015)
Lawless (2004 TV Movie)
Litterpicker (2008)
Living Starts Here (2008)
Location, Location, Location (2000)
Mark of the Wolf (2008–)
Max & Paddy's Road to Nowhere (2004–)
Mayfly (I) (2009)
McNally C
Mrs YparaH's Artefact (2014)
My Dead Friends (2015 TV Mini-Series)
My Hero (2006)
My Own Winter (2016)
New Voices (1994–)
New York Dolls in Newcastle (2011 TV Movie)
No More Cry: The Corrs in Newcastle (2001 TV Movie)
No Place (2005)
Noctambule (2012)

Notice (2016)
Omnibus (1967–2003)
On the Night of the Fire (1939)
One Night in Turin (2010)
Only Human (2005–)
Our Friends in the North (1996 TV Mini-Series)
Out of Reach (1980)
Outsiders (2012)
Papierowe malzenstwo (1992)
Payroll (1961)
Per Mare, Per Terram (2010)
Pet Shop Boys: A Life in Pop (2006 TV Movie)
Pet Shop Boys: Pop Art - The Videos (2003 Video)
Points North (1958–1964)
Princess from Kathmandu (1991)
Purely Belter (2000)
Quayside (1997–)
Question Time (1979–)
Rag Nymph (1997–)
Reggie the Cartoon Character (1984)
Remedy Live (2005 Video)
Rocco Paris (2004)
Ross Noble: Randomist (2006 Video)
Roulette (2004)
Roy Chubby Brown: Jingle Bx@!cks (1994 Video)
Roy Chubby Brown: Pussy & Meatballs (2010 Video)
Run for Me (2008)
Run (II) (2014)
Salvage Squad (2002–2004)
Sarah Millican: Home Bird Live (2014)
School for Seduction (2004)
Second Class Citizen (II) (2012)

Top right: *Josh Duhamel said Newcastle was one of the most beautiful cities he'd ever seen.* Right: *Transformers reek devastation upon Grainger Street.*

Second Thoughts (2013)
Self Made (2010)
Seven Ages of Britain (2003 TV Mini-Series)
Shallow Grave (1994)
Shed Seven: 'What Goes on Tour' (1999)
Shelter (2006)
Shindig! (1964–1966)
Short Changed (2007)
Slow Dance (2008)
Snow White in the Real World (2013)
Song for Marion (2012)
Speaking to Each Other (1988 TV Movie)
Spender (1991–1993)
Spoof! (2004–)
St Mercedes Day (2003)
Staggered (1994)
Stormy Monday (1988)
Strange Wood (2005)
Sublimate (II) (2016)
Suite for Two (2003)
Sunday for Sammy 2004 (2004 Video)
Superstars (1996)
Tapping a Blast Furnace (1899)
The Alan Shearer Story (2005 TV Movie)
The Bad Samaritan Must Die! (2012)
The Bill (1984–2010)
The Black Candle (1991 TV Movie)
The Clouded Yellow (1950)
The Dumping Ground (2013–)
The Dwelling Place (1994 TV Mini-Series)
The Fast Show (1994–2000)
The Fifteen Streets (1989 TV Movie)

The Gallifreyan Candidate (2009 Video)
The Glass Virgin (1995 TV Mini-Series)
The Great Diversion (2017)
The High Life (2009)
The Likely Lads (1976)
The Loss of Sexual Innocence (1999)
The Nail File: The Best of Jimmy Nail Video Collection(1997 Video)
The Name Makers (2003)
The Nightmares Next Door (2005 TV Movie)
The One and Only (2002)
The Other Child (2013 TV Movie)
The Other Possibility (2007)
The Owner (2012)
The Playground (2007)
The Premiership (2001–2004)
The Rise (2012)
The Sanctuary (2014)
The Shouting Men (2010)
The Stables (2004–)
The Wingless Bird (1997 TV Mini-Series)
The World Cup: A Captain's Tale (1982 TV Movie)
Those Were the Days (2008–)
Today I'm with You (2010)
Together (IV) (2013)
Tolerance (2007)
Torpedo Boat Destroyer 'Viper'(1900)
Tracy Beaker Returns (2010)
Tyne & Wear Metro: The Musical (2011 Video)
UFC 80: Rapid Fire (2008 TV Special)
Unconditional (II) (2012)

Unidentified Flying Oddball
(1979)
United! (2011)
Vera (2011–)
Viz: The Documentary (1990
Video)
Walls (II) (2010)
Ways to Live Forever (2010)
We Are History (2000–2001)
We Are Not Like Them (2013)

Westenders (2003–2004)
Women in Tropical Places (1989
TV Movie)
WWE Insurrextion (2003 TV
Special)
Youth of Today (2012)
Zombie Women of Satan 2 (2017)

The story of Keith Crombie, owner of the Jazz Cafe, Pink Lane.

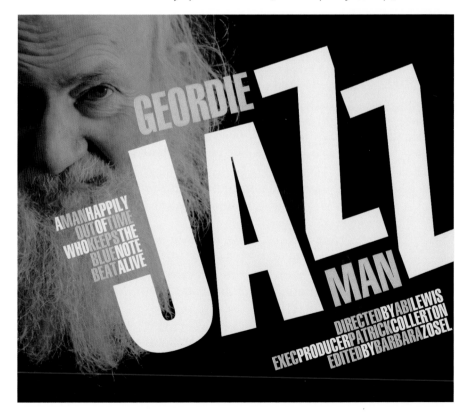

Closing Credits

The author would like to thank the people who made contributions to this book, their insights into filming in Newcastle are invaluable and add an extra, personal dimension to the book. Many took time from their busy schedules to be interviewed by the author.

Andrew Bainbridge - Location Manger, *Vera*

Rob Burrows - Founder Solarus Films

Rob Byron - musicologist and proprietor of Steel Wheels Records, Newcastle

Victoria Elliot - Actress known for *Hebburn* (2012), *Emmerdale* (2010) *The Kennedys* (2015), *55 Degrees North* (2005) and the *Get Carter* stage play (2016)

Peter Flannery - playwright and screenwriter. Resident playwright at the Royal Shakespeare Company in the late 1970s and early 1980s. Notable plays during his tenure include: *Savage Amusement* (1978), *Awful Knawful* (1978), and *Our Friends in the North* (1982). Other theatre work has included *Singer* (1989). Also known for *The Devil's Whore* (2008, Channel 4), *The One and Only* (2002), *Funny Bones* (1995) and *George Gently* (BBC 2005-2017)

Lee Hall - playwright and screenwriter. *Billy Elliot* (2000), *Gabriel and Me* (2001), *Pride and Prejudice* (2005), *The Wind in the Willows* (2006), *Toast* (2010), *War Horse* (2011).

Charlie Hardwick - actress best known for playing Val Pollard from 2004 to 2015 in the ITV soap opera *Emmerdale*. For this role, she won the 2006 British Soap Award for Best Comedy Performance.

Simon Heath - writer *Byker Grove*, recently producer on *The Secret Agent* (2016), *Line of Duty* (2016) and *Dark Angel* (2016)

Bryn Higgins - producer, writer and director with many British TV and film Credits. Including *Unconditional* (2010), *Electricity* (2014) and *Endeavour* (2016)

Melanie Hill - actress, best known for playing Aveline in *Bread* (1986–1991). Also - *Playing the Field* (1998–2002), *Waterloo Road* (2012–2015), *The Syndicate* (2015) and *Coronation Street* (2015–present)

Dave Johns - a stand-up comedian, writer and actor. He has appeared on *Never Mind the Buzzcocks* (four times), *8 Out of 10 Cats* and as God on *Harry Hill*. He starred as the title character in the Palme D'Or-winning Ken Loach film *I, Daniel Blake*.

Ian La Frenais - writer best known for his creative partnership with Dick Clement. Most famous for television series including *The Likely Lads*, *Whatever Happened to the Likely Lads?*, *Porridge* (and its sequel *Going Straight*), *Lovejoy* and *Auf Wiedersehen, Pet*.

Bill Lancaster - Northumbria University, Faculty of Arts, Design and Social Sciences.

Christine Llewellyn-Reeve - location manager, production location manager and producer. *The One and Only* (2002), *Billy Elliot* (2000) *Our Friends in the North* (1996).

Ken Loach - film and television director. Known for his socially critical directing style, which are evident in his film treatment of social issues such as poverty, homelessness *Cathy Come Home* (1966) and labour rights *Riff-Raff* (1991) and *The Navigators* (2001). Loach's film *Kes* (1969) was voted the seventh greatest British film of the 20th century in a poll by the British Film Institute. Two of his films, *The Wind That Shakes the Barley* (2006) and *I, Daniel Blake* (2016) received the Palme d'Or at the Cannes Film Festival, making him the ninth filmmaker to win the prestigious award twice.

Miriam Phipps-Bertram - Journalist and marketing consultant

Tim Prager - television and film writer. (*Dalziel and Pascoe*, *Dangerfield*, *The Ambassador*, *Silent Witness*). He has created three series for the BBC: *Safe and Sound, Two Thousand Acres of Sky* and *55 Degrees North*. His feature-length credits include *The Maid* with Martin Sheen and Jacqueline Bisset; *If the Shoe Fits* starring Rob Lowe and Jennifer Grey; *Haunted* with Aidan Quinn, Anthony Andrews, Kate Beckinsale and Sir John Gielgud; *Vendetta* with Christopher Walken; *Partners in Action* with Armand Assante.

Brian B. Thompson - BAFTA-nominated British television, theatre and radio writer whose work includes *Byker Grove, Grafters, The Bill* and *Coronation Street*. He co-created the Newcastle soap *Quayside*. Theatre includes *Derby Day* (London Fringe Awards, Best Comedy)

Gareth Williams - Location Manager (*Wolfblood, The Dumping Ground, Tracy Beaker Returns, Wire in the Blood*)

Chris Phipps was the BBC's Black Country Correspondent in the 1970s. He moved to the North East to produce Channel 4's flagship rock show *The Tube* from Tyne Tees Television in Newcastle from 1982 to 1987. Since then his passionate and expert knowledge of entertainment and popular music has been captured on radio, television, film, print and the speaker's rostrum.

His ITV series *Northstars* and documentary *Chris Rea - Hard Is The Road* both received prestigious Royal Television Society Awards. This is his second book.